Securing Cloud Services

A pragmatic approach to security architecture in the Cloud

Securing Cloud Services

A pragmatic approach to security
architecture in the Cloud

LEE NEWCOMBE

IT Governance Publishing

Every possible effort has been made to ensure that the information contained in this book is accurate at the time of going to press, and the publisher and the author cannot accept responsibility for any errors or omissions, however caused. Any opinions expressed in this book are those of the author, not the publisher. Websites identified are for reference only, not endorsement, and any website visits are at the reader's own risk. All websites identified were correct and functioning at the time of writing; the publisher and author can take no responsibility for changes since this time. No responsibility for loss or damage occasioned to any person acting, or refraining from action, as a result of the material in this publication can be accepted by the publisher or the author.

Apart from any fair dealing for the purposes of research or private study, or criticism or review, as permitted under the Copyright, Designs and Patents Act 1988, this publication may only be reproduced, stored or transmitted, in any form, or by any means, with the prior permission in writing of the publisher or, in the case of reprographic reproduction, in accordance with the terms of licences issued by the Copyright Licensing Agency. Enquiries concerning reproduction outside those terms should be sent to the publisher at the following address:

IT Governance Publishing
IT Governance Limited
Unit 3, Clive Court
Bartholomew's Walk
Cambridgeshire Business Park
Ely
Cambridgeshire
CB7 4EA
United Kingdom

www.itgovernance.co.uk

First published in the United Kingdom in 2012
by IT Governance Publishing.

ISBN 978-1-84928-396-0

PREFACE

Cloud Computing represents a major change to the IT services landscape. For the first time enterprise-grade computing power is available to all, without the need to invest in the associated hosting environments, operations staff or complicated procurement activities. But this flexibility does not come without compromise or risk.

Security is often cited as one of the major concerns of Chief Information Officers (CIOs) considering a move to Cloud-based services. The aim of this book is to provide pragmatic guidance on how organisations can achieve a consistent and cohesive security posture across their IT services – regardless of whether those services are hosted on-premise or hosted on a Cloud.

This book provides an overview of security architecture processes and how these may be used to derive an appropriate set of security controls to manage the risks associated with working "in the Cloud". This guidance is provided through the application of a security reference model to the different Cloud delivery models of Infrastructure as a Service (IaaS), Platform as a Service (PaaS) and Software as a Service (SaaS).

Please note that this book is not a hands-on technical reference manual; those looking for code snippets or detailed designs should look elsewhere.

ABOUT THE AUTHOR

Lee Newcombe, PhD, is an experienced and well-qualified security architect. During his career, he has been employed by a major retail bank, one of the Big 4 consultancies and a global systems integrator. His roles have included security assessment, security audit, security design, security implementation, business continuity, disaster recovery, forensics, identity and access management, security monitoring and many other aspects of information assurance. He has worked across various sectors, including the financial services, retail and government, latterly working as the security lead for a major law enforcement programme for the UK Government. Lee has worked within numerous "shared service" environments and Cloud programmes, which included acting as the IT industry security subject matter expert during the early days of the UK Government G-Cloud programme.

He is a TOGAF9®-certified enterprise architect and an Open Group certified Master IT Specialist, and holds numerous security certifications – including CISSP and CCSK. He has full membership of the Institute of Information Security Professionals and is also a long-standing member of the CESG Listed Advisor Scheme. Lee is a named contributor to the *Cloud Security Alliance* guidance and has been writing about, presenting on, and working with Cloud technologies since 2007.

ACKNOWLEDGEMENTS

I could not have produced this book without the help and support of my wonderful (and patient!) family. It's been a fairly long and occasionally frustrating process, but I believe that the end result justifies the time and effort. So, the first on my list of people whose contribution I wish to acknowledge must be my wife, Lynne. Not only did she need to tolerate my hiding/working in the study whilst she prevented our dog from eating our children, but she was also then subjected to reading the first draft of each chapter of this book. If the content of this book is now understandable, and vaguely well formed, then that is down to the efforts of Lynne. Thanks Lynne – I could not have done it without your help.

I must also express my thanks to my old friend and colleague, Jonathan Shelby, for taking the time to read through my drafts and providing a different perspective on the issues that I cover. Thanks Jon – it's much appreciated.

A number of my colleagues at Capgemini graciously volunteered to act as reviewers for this book. So, my thanks to Gill Hughes, Andrew Billington, Umesh Vidwans, Peter Groeneveld, Guy Stephens and Jens Liens for taking the time to read some, or all, of this work and providing me with expert comments, together with a degree of confidence that what I say has value. I would also like to thank the reviewers sourced by my publisher (ir. H.L. (Maarten) Souw RE, Enterprise Risk and QA Manager, UWV, Giuseppe G. Zorzino CISA CGEIT CRISC, Lead Auditor 27001, Security Architect and Antonio Velasco, CEO, Sinersys Technologies) for their valuable feedback.

Acknowledgements

Finally, thank you to Angela Wilde, and all at IT Governance, for giving me the opportunity to publish this work.

CONTENTS

Contents

Part One: Introduction

Part one provides the foundation for the rest of this book, as it introduces the concepts embodied within Cloud Computing, describes the associated security threats, and lists a few of the existing industry initiatives dedicated to improving the security of Cloud services.

Part two introduces a number of security architecture concepts and a conceptual security reference model. This model is then applied to the different Cloud service models of Infrastructure as a Service (IaaS), Platform as a Service (PaaS) and Software as a Service (SaaS), showing how the conceptual security services within the reference model can be delivered for each model.

If you are already familiar with Cloud Computing models, terminologies and associated risks, then you could go straight to Part two – although you may find the contents of Part one a useful refresher.

CHAPTER 1: INTRODUCTION TO CLOUD COMPUTING

Cloud Computing: one of the more evocative labels for an IT delivery model – certainly more so than the "utility computing" label, to which Cloud owes much of its heritage. However, like its rain-bearing namesake, Cloud Computing can be difficult to describe, with many observers having their own perspective on what is, and what isn't, Cloud. Many people use Cloud services without realising that they are doing so; iTunes, Hotmail, Facebook and Twitter are all examples of Cloud services. However, these are consumer Cloud services, which are aimed at individual users; the security of such consumer services is not discussed within this book.

The purpose of this book is to help those organisations looking to implement those Cloud services aimed at the enterprise SalesForce services, Amazon Web Services (AWS) and Windows® Azure, for example – and to help them do so both in a risk-managed manner and in accordance with their appetite for risk.

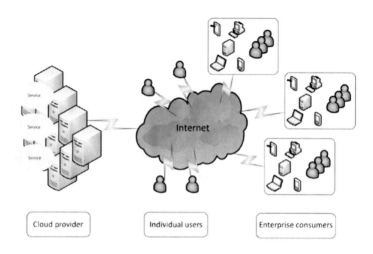

Figure 1: Overview of the Cloud Computing concept

Figure 1 shows a high-level representation of the Cloud Computing model. On the left, we have a Cloud Computing provider – essentially a set of servers offering some form of shared IT service. On the right, we have a set of organisations with users and client devices capable of accessing that shared service. In the middle, we have the Internet (or some other delivery network), which acts as the transport mechanism enabling the access devices to connect to the shared service. You can also see some individual users sitting on the Internet, who are just as capable of accessing those shared services as the larger organisations. The shared service on offer could be anything from the Amazon Web Services model of access to compute and/or storage resources, through to the SalesForce, Huddle or Yammer model of access to specific software applications.

Regardless of the service on offer, there are a number of key characteristics that the service must display in order to be truly "Cloud":

- **Multi-tenant:** The service should (at some level of the technology stack) be shared amongst its users, rather than dedicated to the use of a single consumer. In the case of such services as Amazon Web Services, the multi-tenancy is at the level of the physical hardware and the hypervisor[1], which can host virtualised images serving many consumers. In the case of such services as Salesforce, the multi-tenancy sits at the application level – many different consumers access the same instance of the applications on offer. Consumers are, therefore, separated only by the barriers implemented by the provider. Multi-tenancy is a prime differentiator between Cloud services and more traditional outsourcing models, where resources would more typically be dedicated to individual clients.
- **Ubiquitous network access**: The service should be available to all over a common network. For Public Cloud services, the common network is usually the Internet. For other types of Cloud services, more closed networks – such as government or academic networks – can be used.
- **Elastic:** The service should be able to respond quickly to spikes in demand. The Cloud consumer should be able to add the additional resources needed to maintain service levels during a spike in demand, and then rapidly release them again once the spike has passed.

---

[1] Hypervisors are responsible for the allocation of physical hardware resources – such as compute, storage and communications – to virtualised operating system guests hosted on that hardware.

Cloud providers should look to reduce the amount of manual effort required by consumers to support this elasticity.

- **Pay per use:** Consumers should be charged for the resources that they actually consume; in the case of infrastructure services, the charge could be calculated according to CPU usage per hour, or according to the GB of data stored or transferred. For Cloud providers offering software as a service, it could involve charging per user per month, rather than charging on the traditional basis of a perpetual license.

- **On-demand self-service:** Consumers should be able to provision the services they need themselves, without needing to talk to the Cloud provider. With many popular Cloud services, customers can obtain the services they need with only a network connection and a credit card.

That is my view of Cloud – a view heavily influenced by a particularly popular definition of Cloud produced by the American National Institute of Standards and Technology (NIST). The NIST definition of Cloud Computing is discussed in much more detail in *Chapter 2*. There are a number of services that seek to use the Cloud label, but do not display all of the characteristics described above. A number of service providers have jumped onto the Cloud bandwagon by re-labelling as "Cloud services" those services that would normally just be viewed as shared services. This re-labelling is so common that it has earned its own title: "Cloud-washing".

This book is not dogmatic about whether or not a Cloud service displays all of the expected characteristics, and the guidance it provides is also generally applicable to wider classes of shared services.

CHAPTER 2: OVERVIEW OF EXISTING CLOUD TAXONOMIES AND MODELS

Chapter 1 provided an informal introduction to the main concepts underlying the Cloud Computing model. This chapter provides a more formal set of definitions and introduces common terminology to enable a shared understanding of what is meant when I use such terms as "Infrastructure as a Service", "Community Clouds" and "deployment models".

There are a number of different definitions of Cloud Computing, but the mostly widely accepted is probably that produced by NIST[2]. The NIST definition describes Cloud Computing as being:

... a model for enabling ubiquitous, convenient, on-demand network access to a shared pool of configurable computing resources (e.g. networks, servers, storage, applications, and services) that can be rapidly provisioned and released with minimal management effort or service provider interaction. This cloud model promotes availability and is composed of five essential characteristics, three service models, and four deployment models.

---

[2] *http://csrc.nist.gov/publications/nistpubs/800-145/SP800-145.pdf.*

The five essential characteristics, as defined by NIST, are:

- On-demand self-service
- Broad network access
- Resource pooling
- Rapid elasticity
- Measured service.

The three service models defined by NIST have the familiar labels of "Infrastructure as a Service" (IaaS), "Platform as a Service" (PaaS) and "Software as a Service" (SaaS). These service models will be described in more detail shortly.

The four deployment models identified within the NIST definition comprise those familiar terms of "Public" and "Private" Clouds, together with the less commonly used models of "Community" and "Hybrid" Clouds. Each deployment model is described more fully a little later in this chapter.

There are some interesting things to note about the NIST model of Cloud Computing, one of which is that it focuses on the three main delivery models of IaaS, PaaS and SaaS. In these days of "everything as a service", it is sometimes worthwhile to go back to the basics of IaaS, PaaS and SaaS. Whilst this book is relevant to Business Process as a Service (BPaaS) too – and indeed the other myriad *aaS offerings – it is structured so as to consider each of IaaS, PaaS and SaaS in turn. Those deploying models other than IaaS, PaaS and SaaS should take the relevant guidance and adapt it to their purposes.

Service models

Infrastructure as a Service (IaaS)

In their definition, NIST describe Cloud IaaS as the model where:

The capability provided to the consumer is to provision processing, storage, networks, and other fundamental computing resources where the consumer is able to deploy and run arbitrary software, which can include operating systems and applications. The consumer does not manage or control the underlying cloud infrastructure but has control over operating systems, storage, deployed applications, and possibly limited control of select networking components (e.g. host firewalls).

The most popular example of an IaaS offer is Amazon Web Services. However, there are also many major systems integration companies – such as IBM, HP, CSC and Capgemini – that offer IaaS more specifically targeted at enterprise users.

An example of a more focused IaaS would be Storage as a Service (offered by Nirvanix, for example). Using such a service, organisations (or individuals) can store or archive data in a Cloud-based system, rather than hosting it locally. Another example of IaaS is "desktop as a service", whereby end-users can access their company "desktop" over the Internet; the desktop infrastructure itself would be hosted within a Cloud provider and shared with other clients.

The primary selling point of IaaS is that the Cloud provider has already invested in providing the infrastructure, and so end-user organisations only have to concern themselves with the operational expenditure of using the service, rather than the capital expenditure of building their own services. Consumers, therefore, pay only for the capacity that they actually use – and not for servers sitting idling in their data centres. Furthermore, IaaS promises speedier deployment of new resources, with new server images being available to consumers in a matter of minutes – rather than months, as may be the case for those organisations needing to manage complex procurement and deployment processes. Should demand recede, those resources can then be released again – at which point, the organisation bears no further costs (a marked contrast to the traditional model). IaaS also promises to release headcount currently assigned to physical server management to tasks that offer more perceived value to the business.

At present, the primary use cases for IaaS within the enterprise are for development and test services and for those applications that require significant (but short-term) number crunching, such as market simulations or scientific analysis. Large pharmaceutical organisations are known to use IaaS for numerical modelling purposes, due its superior speed to operation (as compared with the lengthy traditional process of procuring and installing physical hardware).

Few enterprises are adopting IaaS for mission-critical production services at this time. There are a number of reasons for this, with security being one of the dominant factors. Other factors include:

- It is usually more expensive to run a 24/7 service with relatively constant levels of demand on the Cloud. Clouds tend to be cheaper for short-term or bursty applications; consistent loads can often be more cheaply managed on-premise.

- Applications with high input/output requirements may perform less well when hosted on a Cloud service. Furthermore, if an application requires substantial data transfers into and out of the Cloud provider, the cost may be greater than initially anticipated.

Platform as a Service (PaaS)

NIST describes Cloud Platform as a Service as the model where:

The capability provided to the consumer is to deploy onto the cloud infrastructure consumer-created or acquired applications created using programming languages, libraries, services, and tools supported by the provider. The consumer does not manage or control the underlying cloud infrastructure including network, servers, operating systems, or storage, but has control over the deployed applications and possibly configuration settings for the application-hosting environment.

The most well known examples of Platform as a Service include Windows® Azure, Google App Engine® and the Force.com platform.

PaaS offerings build on the advantages of the IaaS model by taking away the overhead of server administration from consuming organisations. Developers get direct access to the development environment and can increase or decrease their compute resources as and when they need; project delivery is no longer dependent on server installation lead times.

As we shall see later in the book, PaaS is, perhaps, the hardest of the three delivery models to secure, as the responsibilities for the delivery of security services are distributed across the provider and consumer much more widely than in the other two service models.

Cloud interoperability and portability is the subject of many industry initiatives[3] – including those by the Open Group[4], the Distributed Management Task Force (DMTF)[5] and the IEEE[6] – but the potential threat of lock-in is more pronounced with PaaS than with either IaaS or SaaS. Most PaaS providers will offer optimised development libraries and APIs[7] that are not compatible with those offered by other providers or traditional products. In practice, this makes it very expensive to move from one PaaS provider to another, as the developed application must be re-coded (ported) to run on the platform offered by the alternative provider.

The PaaS model tends to be very attractive to organisations, such as start-ups, which need quick delivery of Internet-facing services, but may not have the resources to host or manage their own servers at the operating system level.

Software as a Service (SaaS)

NIST describes Cloud Software as a Service as the model where:

The capability provided to the consumer is to use the provider's applications running on a cloud infrastructure. The applications

---

[3] *http://cloud-standards.org/wiki/index.php?title=Main_Page.*
[4] *www.opengroup.org/cloudcomputing/.*
[5] *http://dmtf.org/standards/cloud.*
[6] *http://standards.ieee.org/develop/project/2301.html.*
[7] Application Programming Interface.

are accessible from various client devices through either a thin client interface, such as a web browser (e.g. web-based e-mail), or a program interface. The consumer does not manage or control the underlying cloud infrastructure including network, servers, operating systems, storage, or even individual application capabilities, with the possible exception of limited user-specific application configuration settings.

Without doubt, the most famous example of a SaaS provider is Salesforce.com – a company that offered Cloud services before the term itself was coined. Other examples of SaaS include SuccessFactors.com, Google Docs, Huddle.net and many, many more.

With SaaS, organisations will typically access a specific software application (such as a customer relationship management application) via a web browser. This means organisations only need to consider the business usage of applications and the provision of devices capable of accessing the Internet; concerns about servers, operating systems and application development are no longer relevant. This model can be very attractive to business executives, particularly if the relationship between business and IT representatives has been strained due to past perceptions of poor or unresponsive IT delivery.

The SaaS model is probably the most commercially successful of the three delivery models, perhaps in part due to the previous industry flirtation with the Application Service Provider (ASP) model. Enterprises appear to be more comfortable making use of specific services hosted in the Cloud than they are with the idea of making more general-purpose use of Cloud-based services. SaaS can appear to offer genuine business-enabling services, whereas

PaaS and IaaS may appear to be simply different ways of doing IT.

There are a number of specific, security-focused SaaS offerings, including e-mail security, web content filtering, Authentication as a Service, vulnerability assessment and others. These SaaS offerings are often pitched as providing security expertise for those organisations that cannot provide such expensive expertise internally.

Deployment models

Public Cloud

The Public Cloud model is the archetypal Cloud model; the services are open to all-comers, individuals, enterprises, governments, your collaboration partners and your competition. The key point is that there are no real security barriers governing who can register to access the shared service. The low barrier to entry (typically a requirement for a credit card and an Internet connection) is one of the major selling points of the Public Cloud model.

NIST define a Public Cloud as one where:

The cloud infrastructure is provisioned for open use by the general public. It may be owned, managed, and operated by a business, academic, or government organization, or some combination of them. It exists on the premises of the cloud provider.

Examples of Public Clouds include Amazon Web Services, Windows® Azure, Salesforce.com and most other well-known Cloud services.

Private Cloud

The term "Private Cloud" refers to one of the more contentious concepts within the area of Cloud Computing. Some commentators, such as Werner Vogels of Amazon[8], have argued that Private Clouds do not exist – with the implication that those organisations that believe they have a Private Cloud have only, in fact, a virtualised data centre. I must admit that the distinction between a virtualised data centre and a Private Cloud can be hard to define; however, I do see merit in the idea of a Private Cloud. Whereas, in the Public Cloud, the economies of scale are realised through the sharing of resources – such as CPU cycles and storage – across different organisations, in the Private Cloud, the economies of scale come from the sharing of resources across different cost centres *within* the hosting organisation. Of course, in the Private Cloud model there are much lower savings on capital expenditure than in the Public Cloud, as the hosting organisation must still invest in the IT and physical hosting infrastructure. However, a Private Cloud is still likely to be cheaper to operate than a more traditional infrastructure, due to the smaller impact of a shared, multi-tenant (between cost centres), virtualised IT estate. The perception that Private Clouds are more secure than their Public equivalents is one of the main drivers behind organisations building their own Clouds. These ideas will be explored later in this book.

---

[8] *www.ciozone.com/index.php/Cloud-Computing/Beware-of-the-Private-Cloud.html.*

NIST define a Private Cloud as one where:

The cloud infrastructure is provisioned for exclusive use by a single organization comprising multiple consumers (e.g. business units). It may be owned, managed, and operated by the organization, a third party, or some combination of them, and it may exist on or off premises.

Community Cloud

Community Clouds form the middle ground between Public and Private Clouds – the equivalent of gated communities in areas of high crime. Community Clouds are only open to those members of a community that complete rigorous registration procedures. For those who have been granted access to the community, there would typically be a set of minimum-security controls that member organisations must implement in order to protect the overall community. Community Clouds are more cost effective than Private Clouds, as the cost of building and operating the services are shared across all of the organisational tenants.

NIST define Community Clouds as being those where:

The cloud infrastructure is provisioned for exclusive use by a specific community of consumers from organizations that have shared concerns (e.g. mission, security requirements, policy, and compliance considerations). It may be owned, managed, and operated by one or more of the organizations in the community, a third party, or some combination of them, and it may exist on or off premises.

Secure Government Clouds, open only to departments and their executive agencies, are good examples of Community Clouds.

Hybrid Cloud

NIST define the Hybrid Cloud model as one where:

The cloud infrastructure is a composition of two or more distinct cloud infrastructures (private, community, or public) that remain unique entities, but are bound together by standardized or proprietary technology that enables data and application portability (e.g. cloud bursting for load balancing between clouds).

The main reason for implementing a Hybrid Cloud model would be to ensure that spikes in demand that may exhaust the resources available to a more private deployment model can be more effectively managed. For example, organisations hosting a Private Cloud could draw upon the CPU resources of a Public Cloud, should demand become too great for the Private Cloud to cover. In my opinion, Hybrid Clouds represent the worst of all options from a security perspective; organisations must now consider all security issues for both the Private and Public Cloud models. For example, if an organisation with a Hybrid Cloud is subject to specific compliance requirements (e.g. PCI-DSS or data privacy), they must ensure that these requirements are met in both the Private and the Public Clouds. Difficult problems must, therefore, be solved twice, and will quite likely require different solutions, depending on the specific Cloud services adopted. The one obvious security advantage of the hybrid approach is the likely improved availability of services provided by the additional capacity hosted on the more public Cloud service. As an example, a number of charities burst to Public Cloud services to manage huge spikes in demand following major disasters.

The NIST definitions may be the most widely accepted, but that does not mean that they are the only set of definitions. As you would expect, the analyst firms, such as Gartner, IDC and Forrester, have all produced their own definitions for Cloud Computing and/or Cloud services. I am not going to detail each of the competing definitions for Cloud services (Google can help you find them if you feel the need); I believe that the NIST definitions are now the clear leader, particularly as they have been adopted by cross-industry groups, such as the Open Group and the Cloud Security Alliance.

Jericho Forum® Cloud Cube model

There is one more model that I would like to introduce in this section, and that is the Cloud Cube model, developed by the Jericho Forum®[9]. The Jericho Forum® consists of a group of security thought leaders primarily focused on developing new ways of securing information and data in the modern business environment, where online collaboration with partners, clients and suppliers is commonplace. The Cloud Cube model, shown in *Figure 2*, uses four dimensions to describe different Cloud formations.

---

[9] *www.opengroup.org/jericho/cloud_cube_model_v1.0.pdf*.

The axes of the cube represent three dimensions:

- Internal versus external
- Proprietary versus open, and
- Perimeterised versus de-perimeterised.

The fourth dimension of in-sourced versus outsourced Cloud is represented within the Cloud Cube model using colour coding.

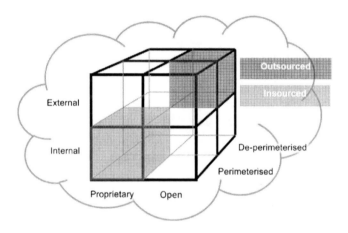

Figure 2: The Jericho Cloud Cube model

The internal/external axis distinguishes between Cloud services hosted within an organisation's own barriers and those hosted outside of those barriers. It should be noted that it is still possible to have an outsourced Cloud hosted within an organisation's own boundary; for example, a service provider could be contracted to build and operate an infrastructure Cloud within an existing data centre. This practice is similar to the traditional outsourcing of IT service management.

The proprietary/open axis refers to the Cloud providers' use of proprietary technologies. The more proprietary the technology offered, the greater the risk of lock-in to the provider the consumers must accept. At present, almost all Cloud providers will gravitate towards the proprietary end of the spectrum; it is really not in their commercial interests to encourage interoperability and portability. However, there are a number of industry initiatives in progress to produce interoperability standards, and so, eventually, there is likely to be a move towards the adoption of open standards.

The perimeterised/de-perimeterised axis refers to the architectural approach adopted by the consumer. If the consumer is still attempting to implement a hard external barrier – albeit a virtualised barrier – then they would still be tending towards the traditional perimeterised model. If the consumer is attempting to offer a service that is geared towards collaboration, and which moves access controls closer towards the data (rather than to the virtual perimeter of the organisation) then it is moving towards the de-perimeterised model.

The Cloud Cube model is a useful tool for categorising Cloud services and, more importantly, in my opinion, for highlighting certain features of Cloud Computing models. For example, a traditional Private Cloud could be viewed as in-sourced, internal, proprietary and perimeterised. However, a Private Cloud could also be outsourced, external, proprietary and perimeterised, if that Cloud service was to be hosted on the Cloud provider's premises, but still dedicated to a single consumer. In this case, there is very little difference between an outsourced Private Cloud and a traditional outsourcing model.

This chapter has introduced the NIST definitions for Cloud Computing. This is important, as the terms IaaS, PaaS, SaaS, Public, Private, Hybrid and Community will be used many times throughout the rest of this book. Now we have a common terminology, let's move on to the security side of things …

CHAPTER 3: THE SECURITY BALANCE

This chapter aims to give a pragmatic overview of some of the potential security benefits and potential pitfalls of working in the Cloud. From the security perspective, working in the Cloud typically tends to be neither intrinsically better nor worse than working on-premise – just different.

Security benefits

Like beauty, security is very much in the eye of the beholder. This is a slightly pretentious way of saying that "good" security is (or at least should be) dependent on the context of your organisation in terms of the nature of your business, the threats and vulnerabilities to which your business is exposed and the risk appetite of your organisation. What is "secure" for one organisation may be viewed as inadequate by another organisation with a lower appetite for risk. Security baselines, therefore, vary across organisations, all of which makes it difficult to make categorical statements about security benefits and downsides. I will, therefore, discuss potential security benefits and downsides; you will have to take an honest look at your current security controls and consider whether each of the following benefits would be a real improvement on your current situation.

3: The Security Balance

Data centre security

Designing, constructing, and then operating a secure data centre is a costly exercise. A suitable location must be found, which will, preferably, be one with a low incidence of natural disasters; be close – but not too close – to transport links; be conveniently located, for staff to commute to work; and have excellent utility facilities for communications, power and water. The data centre must then be constructed, complete with a secure outer perimeter, a secure inner perimeter, appropriate security monitoring devices (CCTV, passive infrared, etc.), strong walls, access control mechanisms (e.g. proximity cards and man-traps), internal monitoring controls and countless other controls. You then need to consider the environmental aspects around cooling, humidity, uninterruptible power supplies, on-site generators (with fuel) and the staff to police and operate the building and the IT hardware that it contains ... or, perhaps, you don't.

Cloud providers have (typically) already invested in state-of-the-art secure data centres. The task of recouping the initial capital expenditure of construction, and the ongoing operational costs, are shared amongst their client base.

For those organisations that do not have adequate data processing environments (e.g. those of you with business-critical servers hiding under that desk in the corner), moving services to a Cloud provider will almost certainly provide a benefit in terms of the physical security of your information assets. For those organisations that already run highly secure data centres, the Cloud will probably not offer much benefit from a security perspective. However, it may prove more cost effective to deploy new applications onto a Public Cloud if capacity issues demand construction of new data centre floor space.

It must be noted that there is an implicit assumption here that the Cloud providers' facilities are as secure as expected; would-be consumers should perform sufficient exercises of due diligence to ensure that they are comfortable with the locations in which their data may be held.

Improved resilience

In most circumstances, it is likely that the top Cloud services will provide more resilience (by default) than the on-premise equivalent. For example, the Windows® Azure platform automatically replicates customer data held within the Azure storage facilities to three separate locations, so as to improve resilience. Amazon Web Services offer a number of different Availability Zones within different Regions, such that services can be hosted across different Availability Zones (or Regions) in order to improve the resilience of the hosted services. Outside of top-tier enterprises, how many organisations have multiple data centres (across different geographies) capable of providing similar levels of resilience? Furthermore, if experiencing a rapid surge in demand, an on-premise service could find itself struggling to cope while awaiting additional capacity to be procured and installed. Additional virtual machine or application instances could be spun up on the Cloud in a matter of minutes (or less, depending upon the provider and toolset).

Of course, not everything always works according to plan, and even Cloud providers have service outages, despite all their efforts to eliminate points of failure. Consumers are well advised to investigate how much information Cloud providers release about past outages, so as to judge their levels of openness and competence in managing incidents. An example of a comprehensive postmortem of the outage of the AWS EC2 service can be found at *http://aws.amazon.com/message/65648/*.

One potential use case for Cloud Computing is disaster recovery. Why invest in a back-up data centre to cater for an event that may never occur, when a Cloud solution could provide an environment to operate within for a short period of time – but at very little cost, whilst not in operation? Whilst full-blown Cloud-based disaster recovery may not be possible for many organisations[10], the Cloud can be a suitable repository for the storage of data back-ups, rather than relying on physical storage media.

Improved security patching

Security patching is not straightforward in many organisations. Firstly, you need to obtain vendor or researcher security advisory notifications, secondly, you need to identify which of those advisories are relevant to your environment, and thirdly, you need skilled staff to understand the content of the bulletins or advisories. Once you are confident that you know you have a problem that you need to fix, you then get into the real pain of patch testing and the scheduling of when these tested patches are to be applied (which is particularly painful if down time is

---

[10] This could be for a number of reasons; for example, Cloud-based disaster recovery would not be possible for organisations running business-critical systems on mainframes that cannot be ported to Cloud services.

necessary to business-critical applications). With SaaS and PaaS (in general), consumers do not need to worry about the patching of operating systems; this task is the responsibility of the Cloud service providers (CSPs). Unfortunately, this is not usually the case for the IaaS model. Here, consumers must still ensure that their virtual images are up to date with the required patches.

SaaS consumers also have the added bonus of not having to concern themselves with patches for the applications that they are using; again, this is the responsibility of the service provider, who would typically patch any issues during their regular updates of functionality, unless there is a need for a more urgent fix. PaaS consumers are responsible for fixing any issues in the code that they may have deployed, whilst the provider is responsible for fixing any issues in the shared capabilities that they offer.

Overall, SaaS and PaaS solutions can significantly reduce the workload of existing system administrators, with regard to the monthly patch process.

Security expertise

Many smaller businesses and start-ups do not have the budget, inclination or identified business need to employ dedicated security staff. A typical large enterprise may require security expertise across a diverse range of technologies, such as networking, operating systems, databases, enterprise resource planning, customer relationship management, web technologies, secure coding and others. It can be difficult and/or expensive for these organisations to retain skilled security staff, due to the demand for such scarce resources.

Most organisations can benefit from the improved security expertise provided when operating in the Cloud. The established Cloud providers are well aware of the impact that a serious security incident would have upon their business in the competitive Cloud market, and so have invested in recruiting and retaining high-calibre security expertise. At the SaaS level, it should be expected that the providers understand the security of their applications extremely well. Similarly, many of the IaaS providers operate customised variants of open source hypervisors, so they, too, should understand the security at least as well as a consumer would understand their own installed hypervisor.

On the other hand, it would be a gross exaggeration to suggest that all Cloud providers operate to the highest levels of security. A study conducted in April, 2011, by the Ponemon Institute and CA[11] canvassed 127 Cloud service providers across the US and Europe on their views with respect to the security of their services. Worryingly, the majority of the surveyed providers did not view security as a competitive advantage, and were also of the opinion that it was the responsibility of the consumer to secure the Cloud – not that of the provider. Furthermore, the majority of the surveyed providers admitted that they did not employ dedicated security personnel to secure their services. Without further details of the providers that took part in this study, it is difficult to judge whether the canvassed providers are truly representative of the Cloud providers targeting enterprise customers. In any case, it is always advisable to investigate the security expertise available to the Cloud provider. This can be done by:

---

[11] *www.ca.com/~/media/Files/IndustryResearch/security-of-cloud-computing-providers-final-april-2011.pdf.*

- Examining any security certifications or independent operational reviews of the service (e.g. SAS70 type II reports[12]).
- Investigating the security materials present on the provider's website, or that is otherwise made available to consumers (sometimes this information is only available under non-disclosure agreements (NDAs)).
- Investigating the security individuals employed by the Cloud provider (e.g. looking for past research papers or thought leadership pieces).

Knowledge sharing and situational awareness

Cloud providers are in a privileged position, in that they have visibility of the network traffic entering, traversing and leaving their Cloud services (with a few exceptions, such as where their consumers are employing encrypted links). This visibility can give the provider the ability to identify an attack against one of their clients and then apply any identified mitigations to the whole of their service, improving the security position of their entire customer base. Although a number of (typically) industry-specific information-sharing exchanges do exist with regard to the sharing of identified attack vectors, such forums tend to be limited in scope, compared to the vista available to the major Cloud providers. Most organisations will, therefore, receive more complete protection when using Cloud solutions than when relying on their own knowledge (or that of their partners) to identify active threats.

---

[12] SAS70 Type II reports examine whether a set of claimed controls are implemented and operated in accordance with the claims. SAS70 is being phased out in favour of ISAE3402 (the international Standard) and SSAE16 (the US equivalent).

There have been a number of occasions on which Cloud providers have informed their clients of a compromise of one of the clients' hosted services, of which the client themselves was unaware. One example of which I am aware involved a compromised virtual server being used to distribute illegal materials. Consumers, therefore, benefit from an additional security monitoring and incident response facility.

Improved information sharing mechanisms

There have been many publicised incidents of sensitive information being placed at risk through the loss of removable storage media, such as flash drives. The Cloud can be a more secure alternative for the sharing of information, particularly when information is encrypted and decrypted on-premise. Consider the balance of possibilities: what is the most likely event – the compromise of the Storage as a Service offer of a major provider, or the loss of a memory stick?

Renewal of security architecture

Moving to any new model of outsourced service provisions should encourage a thorough re-examination of the underlying security requirements of the organisation and/or specific service. Business processes and enabling technologies tend to evolve faster than the deployed security solutions. Consider how many organisations still rely on their stateful inspection firewalls for protection, even though their applications interact using XML tunnelled over TLS (effectively bypassing their firewall).

A fresh start via a move to a Cloud service can offer an opportunity to renew the overall security architecture, such that it supports – rather than hinders – the needs of the business. Even if an organisation decides not to move to a Cloud-based service, this process of re-examination of the security architecture and its underlying requirements can still offer real benefits to the organisation.

Potential pitfalls

As with the potential security benefits of moving to the Cloud, the potential pitfalls are also very much dependent upon the relative merits of the current security solutions in place at the would-be Cloud consumer.

Compliance

Compliance is often highlighted as being one of the major potential problem areas for organisations wanting to make use of Public Clouds. *Chapter 5: Privacy and Data Security Concerns* discusses some of these compliance and regulatory issues in more detail. Suffice to say, for now, that organisations should take great care to ensure that they remain within their compliance and regulatory regimes. Compliance cannot be outsourced.

Assurance

Cloud providers can sometimes make bold claims about the strength of their security controls; however, it can be very difficult to ascertain whether those claims are valid. From the perspective of the Cloud providers, it is clearly not feasible to allow each and every potential customer to conduct a visit and thorough review of the physical security of their data centres. Similarly, the providers cannot afford the resources to be able to answer a multitude of compliance-centred questionnaires for each potential consumer. Consumers should look for those Cloud providers that have undertaken some form of security certification or validation exercise. Examples include ISO27001 certification and the results of a SAS70 Type II audit. Now, in isolation, neither an ISO27001 compliance certificate nor a statement that a SAS70 Type II audit has been undertaken offers much value to consumers. In order to derive any real value from such assessments, would-be consumers must obtain the scope of such exercises, e.g. the statement of applicability for any ISO27001 certification. Such documents are rarely made publically available on the website of the provider, but can sometimes be obtained under non-disclosure agreements. This is clearly not as transparent a process as you would typically find in a more traditional outsourcing agreement.

There are other options for obtaining assurance of the services implemented in the Cloud, these primarily using vulnerability assessment and penetration testing approaches. Amazon Web Services, for example, allows their clients to conduct penetration testing within their own containers, but not across different containers. This does cause concerns for consuming organisations; they may be able to check that their services are correctly configured, but they cannot test the actual barriers separating their virtual environment from those of other tenants within the Amazon Web Services (AWS) infrastructure. Consumers must be comfortable with trusting that the controls in place are effective.

Work is ongoing on the development of assurance methodologies to try and resolve some of these issues. The Common Assurance Maturity Model (CAMM) initiative (*http://common-assurance.com/*) appears to have wide, cross-industry participation. CAMM may eventually provide a common baseline for comparison of the relative strengths of the security controls in place with different Cloud providers.

Availability

In theory, Cloud services should offer greater availability than their on-premise equivalents, due to their greater geographic diversity and wide use of virtualisation. However, to quote Yogi Berra (American Baseball legend): "In theory there is no difference between theory and practice. In practice there is".

Consumers are well advised to closely examine the guaranteed availability service levels stated within the contracts of their likely Cloud providers. Service levels tend to be around the 99.5% mark, with little in the way of recompense should the providers fail to meet those targets.

In the on-premise world, consumers can aim for higher service levels and implement their own measures to ensure those service levels are met, e.g. back-up data centres, uninterruptible power supplies and on-site generators. Just as importantly, organisations can conduct their own disaster recovery exercises, switching across data centres as often as they wish to ensure that the failover processes work correctly. Such testing is not as straightforward for Cloud providers, due to the number of clients potentially having their service adversely affected.

Outages in Cloud services are usually widely reported, and this can give an exaggerated impression of the relative stabilities of Cloud services versus on-premise equivalents. Consider how much press attention is paid to outages in the Microsoft® Office 365 service[13], compared to those outages in the exchange infrastructure of any individual organisation.

For smaller organisations, without the luxury of back-up data centres, the availability offered by Cloud services is likely to be no worse than that available to them on-premise. For large enterprises that have invested in the hardware to support five 9s availability (99.999%), the Public Cloud is unlikely to offer equivalent levels of service for business-critical applications. Private Clouds should be able to meet levels of service equivalent to those of traditional deployments, as the Private Cloud is dedicated to a single consuming organisation.

Organisations considering a move to a Cloud model should confirm any existing rationale underlying expensive high-availability requirements with their business stakeholders prior to discounting the move. It is not uncommon for services to be assigned high-availability requirements "just to be on the safe side", when business stakeholders have not been able to provide more realistic requirements.

Lock-in

Vendor lock-in is a problem with traditional IT, but it's even more pronounced with the Cloud model.

---

[13] For example, *www.theregister.co.uk/2011/09/09/microsoft_cloud_outage/*.

Although significant effort has been invested in improving the interoperability of, and portability between, Cloud services, it is still not straightforward to move an IT service from one Cloud provider to another. At the IaaS level, there is still no widely deployed virtual machine image format amongst Cloud providers. The Distributed Management Task Force's Open Virtualisation Format[14] (OVF) is supported by a number of the well-known hypervisor vendors (e.g. VMWare, XenSource, Dell, IBM, etc.), but has not been widely adopted by public IaaS providers. A cynic could argue that it is not in the commercial interests of IaaS providers to make it straightforward for their consumers to switch providers.

But lock-in is not limited to virtual machine image formats. What about data? Many Cloud provider cost models are designed to make it considerably more expensive to take data out of the Clouds than it is to place data within them. For example, at the time of writing, AWS charges consumers \$0.12 per GB[15] for data transfers out of their Cloud (up to 10TB/month). AWS do not charge for data transferred into their Cloud (not considering the storage costs once the data has been transferred). This becomes more of an issue for any consumers that use an IaaS-hosted application to generate data – in which case, they may have significantly more data to get out than they put in.

The question of data export is also an issue for consumers of PaaS and SaaS services, where data may be stored in specific formats, or, again, be more expensive to export than import. However, data export is not the largest lock-in

---

[14] *www.dmtf.org/standards/ovf.*
[15] This refers to the pricing available from *http://aws.amazon.com/ec2/#pricing* for the EU (Ireland) region on 14th October 2011.

threat for PaaS. Applications must be coded differently to run on different PaaS services – an application coded to run on Windows® Azure would not run on the Heroku® platform, for example. Even where PaaS providers make use of the same underlying language (e.g. C#®, Java® or Ruby), their implementations of the libraries or the APIs available may vary. PaaS consumers must, therefore, be cognisant of the costs involved in porting their applications when considering switching PaaS providers.

Switching between SaaS providers is more straightforward than switching either between IaaS or PaaS providers; consumers need only to be able to export their data from their existing provider and to transform this data into the form expected by a new provider. By "data", I don't just mean business data – such data as audit data and access management information must also be preserved, such that security and/or compliance holes are not created through the switch of providers. Finally, consumers must be aware of the potential impact of switching SaaS providers on the back-end business processes. If an organisation has tailored their business processes to reflect the capabilities of their existing SaaS provider, then changing that provider could require substantial reworking of the relevant business processes. Such a reworking is likely to have an adverse impact upon the dependent business services during the changeover period.

Multi-tenancy

There can be no denying that multi-tenancy adds risk to Cloud services that, for traditional deployment models, are nonexistent. Whether sharing takes place at the data, compute, network or application layer, sharing is still taking place. This means that there is a boundary between your service and those of other tenants that would not be there in a traditional deployment. For a Private Cloud, organisations may not care that different business units now share a boundary. For a Public Cloud, organisations may very much care that they could be sharing a boundary with their most hostile competitors.

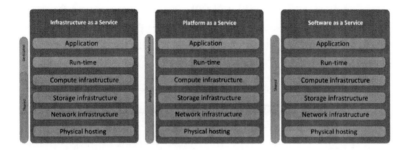

Figure 3: How the level of resource-sharing varies across the service models

Figure 3 illustrates the increasing levels of resource sharing as you move up the IT stack from IaaS through to SaaS.

The issue of multi-tenancy is most commonly discussed at the infrastructure level, particularly with regard to hypervisor security. If an attacker can use a weakness in the hypervisor to jump from their virtual machine into yours, then there is little that you can do to protect yourself. Obviously, hypervisor security is also an issue for any PaaS or SaaS service that relies on server virtualisation to host their services. Hypervisors should not be viewed as security barriers; hypervisors are primarily there to enable organisations to consolidate their physical servers and to offer increased agility in terms of server deployment. Server virtualisation has been subject to extensive research by the security community (e.g. in the work of Joanna Rutkowska et al at *www.invisiblethingslab.com*). Hypervisors have not escaped from such scrutiny unscathed. In 2009, Kostya Kortchinsky of Immunity Security discovered a means of executing code in the underlying VMWare host from a guest machine[16]. This issue was fixed in subsequent releases of the VMWare hypervisor, but the principle was proved: hypervisor hacking could no longer be viewed as just a theoretical threat.

There are many forms of multi-tenancy, each with their own threats. In the case of storage being shared, organisations may need to be aware of the risks associated with iSCSI storage[17]. In the case of back-end databases being shared, organisations need to be comfortable that the security controls within the underlying database are sufficiently strong. For example, SalesForce.com is driven off a single back-end database, with each customer having a specific Organisation ID (OrgID) to use to separate out their data through partitioning[18]. Networks can be shared using a variety of virtualisation technologies; Cisco, for example, offers Virtual Routing and Forwarding (VRF) and Virtual Device Context (VDC) technology, in addition to the well-established Virtual LAN (VLAN) technology. All

---

[16] *www.blackhat.com/presentations/bh-usa-09/KORTCHINSKY/BHUSA09-Kortchinsky-Cloudburst-SLIDES.pdf.*

[17] For example, *www.isecpartners.com/files/iSEC-iSCSI-Security.BlackHat.pdf* (old, but a worthwhile read).

[18] *http://www.developerforce.com/media/ForcedotcomBookLibrary/Force.com_Multitenancy_WP_101508.pdf.*

of this leads to increased sharing of physical network equipment and cabling.

As well as the direct threats to confidentiality posed by attackers breaking through whichever multi-tenancy boundary is relevant to your service model, multi-tenancy also comes with some second-order threats. For example, suppose you share a service with another tenant that undergoes a massive spike in demand (through a distributed denial-of-service (DDoS) attack, for example). The Cloud only gives an impression of infinite resource – there are still physical limits on the compute, network bandwidth and storage availability; such a DDoS could exhaust the available bandwidth, taking out your own service as collateral damage. Another, real-world, example of second-order damage occurred when the FBI suspected a customer of DigitalOne, a Swiss-based service provider, of being related to their investigation of the Lulzsec hacking crew. Rather than simply taking away the three servers suspected of being involved in the illegal activity, FBI agents unwittingly removed three enclosures of servers, effectively knocking several DigitalOne customers off the Internet.[19] Whilst law enforcement seizures of equipment are relatively rare events, they are something that Cloud providers should be able to cater for (e.g. through appropriate disaster recovery mechanisms).

There is no alternative to multi-tenancy in a true Cloud service – it is this level of sharing and increased utilisation of shared resources that drives the underlying economics providing the savings associated with Cloud models.

---

[19] *http://bits.blogs.nytimes.com/2011/06/21/f-b-i-seizes-web-servers-knocking-sites-offline/*.

Cloud consumers need to ensure that they understand where their new boundaries lie when they work in the Cloud, and implement suitable controls to secure – or at least monitor – these new boundaries.

Inflexible and/or inadequate terms and conditions

Most Public Cloud providers offer standard "click wrap" terms and conditions, which users sign up to when they create their accounts. Unless your organisation is of significant scale or importance, there is little opportunity to negotiate individual terms and conditions more suited to your own individual requirements. This is an area where Private and Community Clouds offer more protection and more flexibility than their Public equivalents.

Research by Queen Mary College of the University of London[20] shows that the standard terms and conditions of the major Public Cloud providers typically offer little in the way of protection to the consumer in the event of the provider failing to protect their service or data.

For example, in a survey[21] of Cloud provider terms and conditions conducted by Queen Mary researchers, it was found that " … most providers not only avoided giving undertakings in respect of data integrity but actually disclaimed liability for it". Most providers include terms making it clear that ultimate responsibility for the confidentiality and integrity of customer data remains with the customer. Furthermore, many providers explicitly state that they will not be held liable to their consumers for

---

[20] *www.cloudlegal.ccls.qmul.ac.uk/Research/index.html.*
[21] *www.cloudlegal.ccls.qmul.ac.uk/Research/researchpapers/37188.html.*

information compromise. For example, the *Amazon Web Services Customer Agreement*, updated on 23 August 2011 (*http://aws.amazon.com/agreement/*), disclaims any liability for:

" ... ANY UNAUTHORIZED ACCESS TO, ALTERATION OF, OR THE DELETION, DESTRUCTION, DAMAGE, LOSS OR FAILURE TO STORE ANY OF YOUR CONTENT OR OTHER DATA."

Interestingly, despite the general concern around the location of data within Cloud services, the Queen Mary researchers found that 15 of the 31 providers they surveyed made no mention of the geographic location of data or protection of data in transit between their data centres within their terms and conditions.

One other point worthy of mention with regard to Cloud provider terms and conditions is the recompense available to consumers should their Cloud services become unavailable. Such recompense is usually extremely limited (typically being offered in the form of service credits) and bears no relation to the actual business impact of such an outage on the Cloud consumer. Consumers are, therefore, well advised to maintain tested disaster recovery plans, even when implementing the use of Cloud-based services.

On the positive side, the Queen Mary research found no evidence of Cloud providers attempting to claim ownership of intellectual property that consumers upload to the Cloud. This was an issue that dogged the adoption of Cloud Computing at the outset, and authoritative research in this area is welcome.

CHAPTER 4: SECURITY THREATS ASSOCIATED WITH CLOUD COMPUTING

The previous chapter illustrated some of the potential benefits and pitfalls associated with the security of Cloud Computing. It is worth pointing out that, in the PwC 2012 Global State of Information Security Survey[22], PwC report that the majority of those organisations that have implemented Cloud solutions believe that their move to the Cloud has improved their security.

This chapter highlights some of the threat actors that may be in a position to attack a Cloud-based service. Some of the threat actors discussed in this chapter are taken from the NIST list of important actors for Public Clouds, which is available from *www.nist.gov/itl/cloud/actors.cfm*.

The threat actors discussed in this chapter, and illustrated in *Figure 4*, should be considered during the risk analysis phase prior to any move to a Cloud-based service.

---

[22] *www.pwc.com/gx/en/information-security-survey/giss.jhtml*.

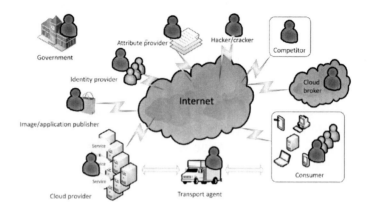

Figure 4: Illustrating the most common threat actors associated with Cloud Computing

Governments do not require a direct connection to a provider to represent a threat to data stored in the Cloud.

Cloud provider staff

Whenever a service is outsourced, the client becomes reliant upon their service provider abiding by the provisions of their agreement. This situation is little different when dealing with Cloud providers; consumers are still reliant upon the Cloud provider to abide by their security commitments. These commitments should include appropriate employment checks, activity monitoring, segregation of duties and internal disciplinary procedures. Cloud consumers are well advised to examine their provider's published staff security commitments prior to trusting their data to them.

Contractual commitments aside, there is still a risk that a member of service provider staff could act maliciously or accidentally to compromise the security of their clients' data. Whilst there are controls – such as on-premise encryption – that clients can implement to protect their data from a compromise of confidentiality, there is little that they can do to protect against risks to availability. Should a privileged member of staff at a service provider turn rogue, there are few technical controls available to prevent them accessing or destroying data, or disabling services.

However, this is also little different to the situation with internally hosted systems; Cloud consumer employees can also turn rogue. There is one factor that may increase the likelihood of Cloud service provider staff turning rogue: threat sources, such as organised crime or intelligence agencies, may be more likely to target Cloud provider staff. These staff may present such threat sources with access to more data or services than any internal staff or employees at more traditional service providers could.

Image/application providers

One of the major productivity benefits of deploying services into the Cloud is the number of pre-configured machine images (e.g. Amazon Machine Images (AMIs)) and applications that are available for almost immediate use. Many AMIs are now available from Amazon themselves, and even more from other EC2 users. These AMIs come with pre-built capabilities for web serving, database hosting, security scanning and many other options.

Security researchers, such as Haroon Meer and his colleagues over at Sensepost, have already demonstrated that it is possible to upload AMIs containing instructions of which the AMI consumers were unaware[23]. Fortunately the Sensepost example simply used wget to obtain a file from Sensepost to allow the researchers to track download and usage of their uploaded AMI. (i.e. the Sensepost researchers could identify whenever their back-doored AMI was used as it contacted their own web servers). It is likely that other back-doored AMIs will be (are?) more harmful in nature.

As well as the threat of purposefully malicious back-doored AMIs, there is also the threat of AMIs that have not been appropriately sanitised prior to being published. Work by Bugiel et al[24] has shown that a large proportion of AMIs contain the "ssh" user authentication key of the AMI publisher. This is dangerous for Cloud consumers, as such authentication keys give the AMI publisher access to the virtual machines of the Cloud consumer. I would surmise that it is most likely that not all of these backdoors were left in by accident. Although I have used the term AMI, the same concerns are relevant to the sharing of pre-built server images for any IaaS provider.

However, trust in the supply chain is not a new issue. Organisations must always place trust in the servers, storage, network equipment and software that they choose to deploy. Organisations will, typically, perform a certain amount of due diligence and testing before purchasing IT assets and then deploying them. This approach should also be adopted before deploying pre-packaged machine images or applications in Cloud-based environments.

---

[23] *www.sensepost.com/labs/conferences/2009/clobbering_the_cloud.*
[24] *www.trust.informatik.tu-darmstadt.de/fileadmin/user_upload/Group_TRUST/PubsPDF/BNPSS11.pdf.*

Competitors

There is nearly always a driver to keep certain information assets away from your competitors. These assets could be your latest findings from research and development, your client list, or something more prosaic – such as your staff directory. When services are hosted internally, organisations can be confident that they understand the barriers preventing access from their competitors.

These barriers become a little less formidable when services are outsourced. IT hardware may still be dedicated to individual clients, but to drive cost-efficiencies, the service desk and support staff may well be shared across the client base of the provider. Similarly, multiple client IT systems may be managed by a common management network and operations centre. Even with a traditional outsourcing arrangement, organisations may find themselves sharing aspects of their service with their competitors.

When moving to a Cloud model, the barriers become even less formidable. An organisation and its competitors could now be operating their services on the same physical servers, having their data stored on the same physical SANs and using the same applications or run-times as their competitors. Competitors may, therefore, see Cloud services as a more likely source of competitive information than more traditional deployment models.

Organisations should, however, bear in mind that the more traditional industrial espionage methods targeted at individuals – such as financial inducements and blackmail – are likely to be just as successful for obtaining information stored on-premise as they are for obtaining information stored within the Cloud.

Crackers/hackers

Crackers have already proven themselves to be a genuine threat to Cloud services – consider the compromise of the Sony PlayStation Network® (PSN)[25] as a prime example. In April 2011, Sony decided to close the PSN whilst they investigated, and recovered from, an attack that had compromised the user account information of millions of PSN users. In May 2011, Sony estimated that this breach of security was going to cost the business around $170 million.

Hackers may pose a more direct threat to services deployed on Cloud systems than to those deployed on-premise. Side-channel attacks may allow an attacker to identify the physical hardware hosting their target's virtual images. The attacker can then attempt to bring up their own virtual machine on the same physical hardware. A hacker would still require a mechanism to then break the virtualisation barrier(s); however, work by Ristenpart et al[26] has shown that the side-channel analysis reconnaissance is not merely a theoretical problem. So, whilst hackers and crackers are a threat to systems wherever they are hosted, more attack vectors exist with respect to services hosted on a Cloud service.

Insiders

Insiders – e.g. company employees – have long been considered by security professionals to be one of the major threat sources to organisations. Insiders tend to be trusted

---

[25] *www.bbc.co.uk/news/technology-13206004.*
[26] *www.cs.tau.ac.il/~tromer/papers/cloudsec.pdf.*

(to some extent), and so granted access to applications and data. Insiders are, therefore, in a position where they could deliberately, or accidentally, release, modify or destroy valuable data. This issue of insider access to data is independent of the IT delivery model, and so is equally applicable to Cloud services.

Cloud does, however, present a new mechanism by which insiders could knowingly, or unwittingly, compromise the data or services of the organisation to which they belong. Cloud services are extremely straightforward to sign up to and use; all that is typically needed is a credit card and an Internet connection. It is, therefore, easy for an insider to deploy a Cloud service and inadvertently open up new mechanisms for business data to be exfiltrated – or for attackers to infiltrate back-end systems.

This is not a new pattern of behaviour; similar behaviours were displayed during the rise of the client/server model and during the early days of wireless networking. Proactive and technology-aware members of staff would implement their own systems or Wi-Fi networks, as they found that they could get the IT services they wanted without having to suffer the delays often associated with central IT teams – a phenomenon commonly known as "shadow IT". Cloud Computing displays many similar characteristics to these earlier disruptive technologies: Cloud services can be quick and easy to deploy, promising more efficient delivery of the services required by business users. Unresponsive or overly risk-averse IT departments can, therefore, exacerbate the threat posed by insiders establishing their own shadow IT services.

Governments

Cloud Computing is a global phenomenon. Cloud services are offered from data centres across the world. Many governments have the legal authority to seize data from data centres hosted within their territories. Some governments have even enacted legislation granting them access to data hosted outside their jurisdiction, where the organisation hosting the data concerned has a subsidiary based within their jurisdiction[27]. Such legislation is usually justified as being required for counter-terrorism purposes, or for fighting the distribution of child pornography. Some nations do not attempt to justify their access rights and simply take advantage of their position in order to maintain order within their populations. Often, the service providers are under legal obligations not to inform the data owners of any such data seizure.

One example of a major data seizure is that of the US Government's seizure of payment data from SWIFT, the organisation that facilitates the transfer of funds between banks. It was reported that the US Government compelled SWIFT to provide details of archived inter-bank transfers conducted through SWIFT for the previous four years. The output from the Belgian Commission for the Protection of Privacy's (CPP) investigation of the events can be obtained from: *www.privacycommission.be/sites/privacycommission/ files/documents/03.01.02-swift_decision_en_09_12_2008 .pdf*.

It is clear that the ability of sovereign states to seize data is not limited to data hosted by Cloud service providers.

---

[27] For example, the United States of America has the Patriot Act.

However, it is equally apparent that Governments do represent a threat to the privacy of business data; this threat is simply exacerbated by the Cloud model, where data could be located in more jurisdictions than would be typical with other deployment options.

Transport agents

Some organisations have a requirement to transfer large amounts of data for storage and/or processing at their Cloud provider. The usual mechanism for transferring data between the consumer and the Cloud is the Internet. This is clearly impractical for large datasets. Cloud providers, including GoGrid and AWS, have recognised this limitation, and so offer services whereby consumers can save their data on to a hard drive, and then mail or courier this hard drive to the provider. Consumers taking advantage of this service must, therefore, find a means of getting their hard drives to the Cloud providers – this is the role of the transport agent.

Transport agents, therefore, represent a viable threat to the security of the Cloud consumer's data. They are in possession of a hard drive containing large amounts of consumer data, which may or may not be protected by encryption.

Identity providers

The use of identity federation techniques is a common recommendation of Cloud security papers. Identity federation enables organisations to manage their Cloud users' identities on-premise, and can provide seamless access to applications, whether they are hosted on the

Cloud or on-premise. If organisations do not want to manage their own identities, then they could rely upon public third-party identity providers, such as Facebook, LinkedIn and Twitter, via their support for OAuth or similar standards. Whilst it would be a brave business that relied upon such providers to secure access to their internal systems, a case can certainly be made for using such providers for consumer-facing Internet services. Such a case could be built around improving the end-user experience through providing them with greater control over their personal information. For example, end-users could choose to provide different subsets of personal information to different identity providers, and so prevent any one provider from having access to an overly extensive set of personal data.

If an organisation makes the choice to use an external identity provider to secure a Cloud-based application, then they must recognise that a compromised (or malicious) identity provider represents a serious threat to their service.

Attribute providers

Similar arguments to those just expressed with regard to identity providers can be made with regard to attribute providers – providers of specific attributes associated with an identity, that is to say. For example, a user may be authenticated to an application using Facebook Connect, but the application may then require further details associated with that identity to make fine-grained access control decisions. Such details (attributes) can be stored within, and made available by, a different service provider. This can allow an organisation to split authentication and authorisation data, whilst also minimising the effect of a single compromise on the privacy of their end-users. Note: end-users could choose to store a minimum set of data with their identity providers and with each attribute provider, so as to minimise the impact of a compromise of any single provider.

Of course, a compromised (or malicious) attribute provider then represents a threat to the security of the relying application.

Cloud management brokers

Some organisations may want to deliver their IT using a number of different Cloud service providers (in order to benefit from additional resilience or variable pricing, for example). However, they may not want to have to worry about the quirks of each service that they use. The role of the Cloud management broker[28] is to sit between the client and their Cloud services. Brokers can present a single interface for their clients to use to build and operate their services, whilst themselves handling the complexities of actually running these services on a variety of Clouds in the background.

Cloud management brokers are, therefore, in a trusted position and represent a potential threat to organisations making use of their services.

This chapter introduced a number of different entities that could represent a threat to an organisation's Cloud-based services. Knowledge of potential threats enables organisations to build barriers that are effective against the

---

[28] Sometimes known as Cloud Service Brokers or Cloud Brokers.

methods likely to be employed by each relevant threat. Organisations can use the threat descriptions within this chapter to check that the security controls that they have implemented cater for the threats that they have identified as being within scope.

CHAPTER 5: PRIVACY AND DATA SECURITY CONCERNS

Alongside security, compliance with legislative and regulatory requirements ranks as one of the most commonly cited concerns for those considering a move to Cloud Computing.

This chapter provides a brief overview of the data privacy concerns impacting the adoption of Cloud services, primarily those imposed by the European Union through the Data Protection Directive. There is also a brief discussion of mechanisms to achieve compliance with the Payment Card Industry Data Security Standard (PCI-DSS) when operating in the Cloud.

This chapter is not intended to provide comprehensive advice on the legality or compliance status of any particular Cloud solution – organisations should always consult their own legal counsel prior to storing or processing personal data using a Cloud service.

Data protection issues

The area of privacy and data protection is commonly viewed as a major concern by those considering a move to Cloud Computing. Where there is a requirement to keep personal data within specific geographical borders, it's not unreasonable to be concerned when that data seems to disappear into a globally diverse Cloud. Similarly, if you are worried about certain unfriendly governments gaining access to your data, then, again, you will be concerned that your data may find its way into their jurisdictions once it is within the Cloud. This section considers the implications of the EU Data Protection Directive (European Communities Directive 95/46/EC) – in particular, its UK interpretation, the Data Protection Act 1998. Each EU member state has implemented its own national laws to incorporate the provisions of the EU directive. However, each nation may have interpreted the requirements of the directive slightly differently, so whilst the guidance within this section may be more generally applicable, it is biased towards the UK interpretation. Finally: I am not a lawyer. Do remember that organisations should consult their own legal advisors before placing personal data into the Cloud. Once it's gone, it's gone.

That said, I will start with a quick overview of the jurisdiction of Directive 95/46/EC, as there are some important scoping issues worthy of discussion. At present, the jurisdiction of the EU directive is "linked to the use of equipment in EU territory or establishment of the Cloud provider (either as data controller or as data processor) in an EU Member State."[29] So, a Cloud provider established within India and operating data centres in China may be outside of the scope of the directive, even if it targets EU users. The Article 29 Working Party, the European Data Protection Supervisor, and others, are working towards an updated version of the EU directive in order to close this jurisdictional loophole and, therefore, it would be unwise for a provider to rely on this exception in the long term. There is another exemption in the scope of the directive that is relevant to Cloud Computing: the "household"

---

[29] Giovanni Buttarelli, European Data Protection Supervisor, http://docbox.etsi.org/Workshop/2011/201109_CLOUD/01_ToolsAndLegalConcepts/EDPS_BUTTARELLI.pdf.

exemption. This excludes data processing carried out by individuals in the course of purely personal or household activity. This may exempt some of the big-name consumer Cloud services from the scope of the directive (Buttarelli gives the examples of Google and Dropbox). Again, this exemption is likely to be removed during the current review of the EU Privacy Directive.

As a starting point, we need to define some common terms used in data protection discussions[30]:

Data Controller: " … a person who (either alone or jointly or in common with other persons) determines the purposes for which and the manner in which any personal data are, or are to be, processed".

Data Processor: " … any person (other than an employee of the data controller) who processes the data on behalf of the data controller".

Data Subject: "an individual who is the subject of personal data".

Personal Data: " … means data which relate to a living individual who can be identified

a) From those data, or
b) From those data and other information which is in the possession of, or is likely to come into the possession of, the data controller, and includes any expression of opinion about the individual and any indication of the intentions of the data controller or any other person in respect of the individual".

---

[30] Definitions taken from *www.legislation.gov.uk/ukpga/1998/29/section/1*.

5: Privacy and Data Security Concerns

In most circumstances, a Cloud consumer storing or processing the personal data of their staff or customers in a Cloud solution would be the data controller. The Cloud provider would typically be viewed as a data processor. However, this may not always be the case. The EU Data Protection Supervisor has argued in the past that, depending on the level of control of processing offered, Cloud providers could also be acting as data controllers. This is particularly applicable to SaaS providers, who more or less dictate how their customers can process personal data through the services that they offer. This interpretation is yet to be tested in the courts.

For now, we will work with the assumption that Cloud providers are data processors and Cloud consumers are data controllers.

Cloud consumers are, therefore, obliged to protect the personal data that they wish to store or process in the Cloud in line with their relevant data protection legislation. In the UK, the Data Protection Act 1998 (DPA) has eight principles:

1. Personal data shall be processed fairly and lawfully and, in particular, shall not be processed unless:

   a) At least one of the conditions in Schedule 2 is met, and

   b) In the case of sensitive personal data, at least one of the conditions in Schedule 3 is also met.

2. Personal data shall be obtained only for one or more specified and lawful purposes, and shall not be further processed in any manner incompatible with that purpose or those purposes.

3. Personal data shall be adequate, relevant and not excessive in relation to the purpose or purposes for which they are processed.

4. Personal data shall be accurate and, where necessary, kept up to date.

5. Personal data processed for any purpose or purposes shall not be kept for longer than is necessary for that purpose or those purposes.

6. Personal data shall be processed in accordance with the rights of data subjects under this Act.

7. Appropriate technical and organisational measures shall be taken against unauthorised or unlawful processing of personal data and against accidental loss or destruction of, or damage to, personal data.

8. Personal data shall not be transferred to a country or territory outside the European Economic Area unless that country or territory ensures an adequate level of protection for the rights and freedoms of data subjects in relation to the processing of personal data.[31]

I'm only going to discuss those principles that are directly impacted by a move to Cloud Computing services, i.e. Principle 7 (on data security) and Principle 8 (on the international transfers of data). The other principles are no less important, but should already have been considered in any existing processing of personal data. Principle 7 compels data controllers to implement good practice with regard to the security of the personal data that they hold. Cloud consumers should, therefore, consider this legal obligation when they are conducting their due diligence activities with regard to their choice of Cloud provider.

---

[31] Taken from *http://www.legislation.gov.uk/ukpga/1998/29/schedule/1/part/1*.

Cloud consumers should be able to convince themselves (and others) that their chosen Cloud providers have sufficient security controls in place to satisfy the good practice requirements of Principle 7.

The most obviously relevant DPA Principle, when it comes to Cloud Computing, is Principle 8. Principle 8 forbids the transfer of personal data to countries that do not provide a similar level of legislative protection of personal data to that of the EU – unless some form of compensating arrangement is in place. Personal data can, therefore, be transferred freely within the European Economic Area (EEA) and, also, to a number of countries that the EU has approved as having adequate data protection controls (currently Andorra, Argentina, Canada, the Faroe Islands, Guernsey, the Isle of Man, Israel, Jersey and Switzerland). EU-based Cloud consumers storing or processing data within Clouds hosted outside of the EEA must implement one of the approved routes for international data transfer beforehand.

There are a number of options for enabling the international transfer of data outside of the EEA, including:

* The use of binding corporate rules (BCRs)
* The use of model contract clauses provided by the EU[32], and
* An in-house assessment of adequacy.

Organisations wishing to use US-based Cloud providers could also consider making use of a Cloud provider that has

---

[32] *http://eur-lex.europa.eu/LexUriServ/LexUriServ.do?uri=OJ:L:2010:039:0005:01: EN:HTML.*

signed up to the provisions of the Safe Harbor agreement between the US Department of Commerce and the EU. However, such organisations should remember that certain industries (e.g. financial services) are excluded from the provisions of Safe Harbor and, also, that Safe Harbor is a self-certification scheme. Such organisations should also remember that the US Patriot Act trumps the Safe Harbor agreement and, therefore, if US Government access is undesirable, they should not rely upon Safe Harbor to provide protection.

Payment card industry issues

Another common compliance requirement that is often raised in the Cloud context relates to the Payment Card Industry Data Security Standard (PCI-DSS). The PCI-DSS[33] aims to set a minimum baseline of security controls (documented as 12 high-level requirements and significantly more low-level requirements) necessary to adequately secure payment card account data within an organisation.

Each payment card issuer – the likes of Visa, MasterCard, American Express, etc. – defines different tiers of merchants, which are usually categorised by the numbers of payment card transactions performed per year. Each merchant level is subject to different specific audit and reporting requirements. Level 1 tends to be the top tier across the issuers, and so Level 1 merchants face the most stringent audit and reporting requirements. Merchants

---

[33] *www.pcisecuritystandards.org/security_standards/documents.php?document=pci_dss_v2-0#pci_dss_v2-0.*

processing more than six million payment card transactions annually are categorised as Level 1 by Visa and MasterCard[34]. American Express sets the bar significantly lower, at 2.5 million transactions per year, and JCB even lower, at 1 million. American Express[35] also only has three levels of merchants, compared to the four levels of Visa and MasterCard. Some of the PCI-DSS requirements that can cause issues in Cloud deployments include requirements for regular vulnerability assessments and an ability to conduct a physical audit of the hosting environment. Penalties for breach of compliance can include substantial fines (e.g. $500,000 per incident) and even the possible removal of a non-compliant merchant's ability to process cards issued by the affected card issuer(s).

A number of Cloud service providers now claim compliance with PCI-DSS[36]; consumers making use of such services can, therefore, place some reliance in them. However, consumers must ensure that they have complete knowledge of the scope of the provider's compliance, so that a cohesive and demonstrably compliant consumer solution can be implemented. The PCI Security Standards Council have provided a useful supporting guide discussing virtualisation and Cloud aspects of PCI compliance over at *www.pcisecuritystandards.org/documents/Virtualization_In foSupp_v2.pdf*.

---

[34] *http://usa.visa.com/merchants/risk_management/cisp_merchants.html*; *www.mastercard.com/us/company/en/whatwedo/determine_merchant.html*.

[35] *https://www260.americanexpress.com/merchant/singlevoice/dsw/FrontServlet? request_type=dsw&pg_nm=merchinfo&ln=en&frm=US&tabbed=merchantLevel*.

[36] *http://aws.amazon.com/security/pci-dss-level-1-compliance-faqs/* and *www.rackspace.co.uk/media-centre/news/article/article/rackspace-enhances-security-with-pci-accreditation/*.

Organisations could also explore alternative options to the storage of payment card information, such as the use of third-party payment providers. This can remove most of the PCI-DSS burden from the organisation itself, as it will never actually have sight of the data in scope for PCI-DSS.

This book does not set out to develop a generic solution that evidences compliance with PCI-DSS. Rather I'll be showing how security architecture methodologies can be used to result in the production of an architecture that takes account of requirements sourced from PCI-DSS.

Others

This chapter has briefly touched upon data privacy and PCI-DSS issues. This is not an exhaustive set of regulatory or legislative compliance requirements. I believe that the subject is worthy of a series of books in its own right. For example, see the *Bloor Report*, Stanley, 2010, available for download at *www.bloorresearch.com/research/white-paper/2071/EU-Compliance-and-Regulations-for-the-IT-Pro.html*.

This report discusses 33 different sources of regulatory and compliance requirements relevant to IT delivery. And this only includes those relevant to the EU!

Government organisations must also be aware of any specific compliance requirements that have been devised by their own home governments. The US Government, for example, has set up the FedRAMP initiative for Cloud providers looking to service the US administration. Delivery of the FedRAMP standards has been delayed, but they are likely to be influential once established. More details on FedRAMP can be found at *www.nist.gov/itl/cloud/upload/NIST_-FedRAMP_ announcement_content.pdf.*

The best advice is to consult with your legal counsel and compliance colleagues to ensure that all relevant sources of requirements are considered and adequately implemented (in line with your organisational appetite for risk) prior to launching new services.

Part Two: Pragmatic Cloud Security

Part two is the meat of this book, providing pragmatic advice on deploying Cloud services in a risk-managed fashion.

This book uses security architecture techniques to drive a consistent, cohesive and comprehensive approach to securing Cloud services. Part two, therefore, begins with an overview of the security architecture processes that can be used to derive the necessary security controls associated with a proposed Cloud deployment. I then introduce a security reference model (SRM), which provides the basis for the discussion of the delivery of security controls across the different Cloud service models.

CHAPTER 6: INTRODUCTION TO SECURITY ARCHITECTURE

Chapter 6 introduces the concepts of security architecture, drawing on well-established enterprise architecture methodologies to derive logical services that deliver consistent levels of security, regardless of the technologies used to implement those services. One of the main advantages of adopting this approach is the complete traceability from business requirement to technical component. This allows the business to understand how their risks are managed and to understand the consequences of any move to Cloud-based services.

What is security architecture?

The international software architecture standard ISO/IEC 42010[37] defines architecture as, "The fundamental organization of a system, embodied in its components, their relationships to each other and the environment, and the principles governing its design and evolution". Architecture can, therefore, be thought of as an abstract view of a system (or organisation or enterprise) in terms of its component parts and how these parts interact with themselves and the outside world.

By slightly adapting the ISO/IEC 42010 words, we can think of security architecture as "The fundamental security organisation of a system, embodied in its components, their relationships to each other and the environment, and the

---

[37] *www.iso.org/iso/iso_catalogue/catalogue_tc/catalogue_detail.htm?csnumber=50508*.

principles governing its design and evolution". In essence, security architecture should provide a holistic view of the security controls relevant to the enterprise (or solution). Furthermore, the architecture should demonstrate how these controls are adequate for meeting the underlying requirements and identified risks. Conversely, the security architecture should also be able to demonstrate:

- Where requirements or risks are not being adequately managed, and
- Where controls may have been implemented, but do not demonstrably meet a documented requirement or manage an identified risk.

Finally, a fully formed security architecture should be able to identify the physical security components in place at an organisation and, therefore, identify duplicate security services in a drive to consolidate them (thereby reducing ongoing expenditure). The goal of the security architecture should be to enable, and not hamper, the needs of the business.

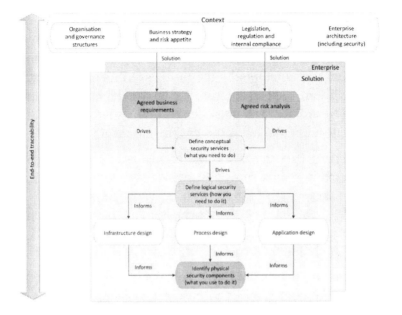

Figure 5: Illustration of the security architecture process

Figure 5 shows how a security architecture process can be implemented. This process is applicable at either individual solution or enterprise levels. For the solution architecture, I would expect any existing enterprise architecture (including security aspects) to form a further element of the Context layer at the top of the figure. This element is dotted within the diagram to reflect the fact that an enterprise security architecture may not be present if deriving such a beast is the aim of the exercise!

The importance of the context layer cannot be overstated. A security architecture must reflect the organisation in terms of its goals, structures and activities, and acknowledge the risk appetite of the business. A security architecture that attempts to enforce an overly risk averse approach on a fairly relaxed business will fail. A security architecture that ignores existing governance structures, and which is derived in an ivory tower will fail. A security architecture that blocks all attempts by the business to meet their stated goals will fail – spectacularly. To stand a chance of success, a security architecture must demonstrate how it fits within an organisation and helps the business to meet its needs.

This is not to say that a security architecture cannot attempt to improve upon existing governance structures, or seek to educate key stakeholders with a view to altering risk appetites. To do this, however, it must include suitable mechanisms for managing such change; it is not enough to simply wish that the context were different.

So, assuming that the security architect is fully versed in the context, the next stage is to ensure that there is an agreed set of business requirements that the organisation is looking to fulfil via the system under consideration. These requirements should also include the key non-functional requirements around service levels (e.g. availability) and hosting. Similarly, the architect should ensure that a risk assessment of the service has been conducted. Both the requirements and the risk assessment must be informed by the context and, crucially, the set of requirements and identified risks must be agreed by the business. This agreement is critical to achieving a successful adoption of the security architecture. The business agreement on the capabilities the security architecture must provide and the risks that it must mitigate helps to smooth the adoption of the security architecture by design teams and, in due course, by the end-user population.

Once a set of requirements and risks has been agreed, it is time for the security architect to use their skills and experience to derive a set of architectural services capable of meeting the needs of the organisation.

What is a service?

What do I mean by the term "architectural service"?

I'll be adopting some of the thinking associated with service-oriented architecture (SOA) to drive the security architecture processes I'm using in this book. So, by "architectural service", I mean a self-contained set of discrete, repeatable, functionality. These chunks of functionality can then be co-ordinated (or "orchestrated", to use the SOA terminology) to deliver flexible capabilities. To put this into a security context, you could consider a security-monitoring capability being provided through an orchestrated set of services, including logging, analysis, reporting and event management services.

Now, unfortunately, I cannot pretend to have invented the idea of security architecture, solution architecture or enterprise architecture. Example enterprise architecture frameworks include the Zachman Framework[®38] and The Open Group Architecture Framework (TOGAF[®])[39], amongst others. In the security space, we have the well-respected Sherwood Applied Business Security Architecture (SABSA[®])[40]. As an aside, work is underway to integrate SABSA and TOGAF, such that SABSA can be used to provide the security elements of an overall

---

[38] *http://zachmaninternational.com/2/Zachman_Framework.asp.*
[39] *www.opengroup.org/togaf/.*
[40] *www.sabsa.org/.*

framework[41]. The methodology I use in this book does not draw directly on any of the processes defined within the aforementioned publications; rather, it draws upon their shared underlying philosophies – such as their aim to increase the alignment of technical IT delivery with the needs of the business stakeholders. But don't worry if you either don't agree with the SOA philosophy or do not have great experience with any of the aforementioned approaches – you should still find some value in the contents of this book.

Architectural layers

I have adopted the layers of abstraction defined within Capgemini's Integrated Architecture Framework (IAF)[42] for use within this book. I have already stressed the importance of agreeing the context of the architecture work. The context layer sits at the top of the stack of architectural layers shown in *Figure 6*.

---

[41] *www2.opengroup.org/ogsys/jsp/publications/PublicationDetails.jsp?publicationid= 12449*.
[42] *www.capgemini.com/insights-and-resources/books/integrated-architecture-framework/*.

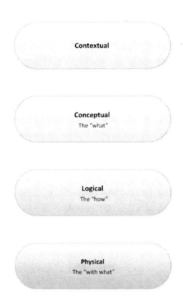

Figure 6: The IAF Architectural Layers

In particular, I believe that the Conceptual, Logical and Physical layers (as shown in *Figure 6*) represent an easily understood route from a defined business requirement through to a defined technical solution.

Conceptual: The "what"

The Conceptual layer of an architecture defines what services are necessary to deliver the outcomes expressed within business strategies, drivers and goals. These services must also be defined in line with agreed architecture principles and other elements described by the context. In the case of a conceptual security architecture, I usually define a set of security services that can be traced back to agreed business requirements, and which aim to mitigate the risks identified by an agreed risk assessment. As an example of a Conceptual security service, let's describe a requirement to only allow authorised access to resources, such as data or applications. In order to prevent unauthorised access to resources, there must, therefore, be some kind of filter in place, blocking such unauthorised access. So, at the Conceptual layer, we can define a Filter service that only allows authorised access to resources. Note that we have not defined what the protected resources are (e.g. networks, operating systems, applications, etc.) or how the Filter service should work – we have only defined what the Filter service must do.

Logical: The "how"

The Logical layer describes how to deliver the conceptual services needed through the derivation of a set of independent logical services and the interactions (contracts) between these services. These logical services remain product-agnostic, but simply define how the overall architecture should work to meet the needs of the business.

In the case of a logical security architecture, I map these logical security services onto the conceptual services, so as to ensure that traceability is maintained. So, to re-visit the conceptual Filter service, we must now consider how a Filter service could work. For this derivation, we'd need to know the resources to be protected and the threats to guard against. At a high level, let's assume that we'd need a logical network filter (to protect against network attacks), a logical operating system filter (to protect against unauthorised use of OS commands) and a database filter (to protect against unauthorised access to data). It's clear, at this point, that we'd also need a whole set of Identity Management and Authorise services to provide the Filter service with the necessary information about the access rights of users to services and data, but I'll keep our example simple for now! Note that these logical security services remain product-neutral – we know how these services should work and the protection that they should provide, but we have not defined the products used to implement them.

Physical: The "with what"

The Physical layer is the layer at which we concern ourselves with the products, processes and application components needed to implement our security services. The Logical layer provides us with a set of functional requirements, non-functional requirements, service levels and interface requirements; the Physical layer defines physical components capable of meeting those requirements.

So, if our Logical layer includes a network filter that must be EAL4 evaluated and able to deliver enterprise-class performance, then we could consider delivering that logical service using a Cisco ASA 5500 firewall (for example).

These physical components can then be mapped onto the logical services, which are then mapped to the conceptual services, which are, in turn, mapped onto the underlying business requirements and risks. We can, therefore, get complete traceability from the business requirements through to the physical component.

The other main point to note is that it is only at the Physical layer that we concern ourselves with actual specific technologies. So, from a Cloud perspective, the conceptual security architecture should be the same, regardless of whether the business service is being implemented on-premise or on-Cloud – the goals and aims for the service are independent of the method of IT delivery. The Logical layer will also often be independent of physical delivery – subject to consideration of the technical feasibility of delivery! What this means is that the Cloud security architect can then concentrate on finding suitable technical means to deliver the necessary security services (to the levels defined at the Logical layer) using appropriate Cloud-relevant components.

Advantages of security architecture

What advantages are offered by following a security architecture approach like the one outlined in this chapter?

Improved traceability from business requirements to security solutions: The security services within an enterprise security architecture are derived from a set of agreed business requirements and the output from an agreed risk analysis. This enables complete traceability between the business requirements (and/or risks) and the security services. Traceability can then be continued through to the physical security product (or process) that implements the architectural security service. This provides an organisation with complete traceability end-to-end: from the initial business requirements to the implemented solution. Such traceability is extremely valuable for managing change and for the purposes of internal, and external, audit.

Improved sponsorship and governance: Sponsorship from senior business stakeholders is essential for the success of any piece of architecture work – including enterprise security architecture. Such sponsorship encourages participation from the wider organisation and helps to enforce implementation.

Improved project success rate: The reuse of security architecture patterns reduces the amount of design work required per project and acts as an accelerator, reducing the overall cost of development. In addition, if an organisation reuses existing physical components, there is less risk of unexpected problems with unfamiliar technologies delaying project implementation.

Reduced risk of breaches of compliance requirements: An enterprise security architecture should incorporate the compliance requirements (legal, regulatory and internal) within the context. This enables the organisation to derive a holistic approach to information security. As the compliance requirements are embedded within the architecture, they flow through into individual solution delivery (Cloud or on-premise), alongside the other business requirements.

Ensures security is embedded at the earliest stage of development: A common problem with project delivery is the late incorporation of security requirements into the project development life cycle and the lack of integration between security architecture and the delivery processes of other architecture domains, such as application, information and technology. This can often lead to expensive design changes and the shoehorning of inappropriate security products into the solution. Through enterprise security architecture, and attendant governance processes, the organisation can ensure that security requirements are considered early in the design life cycle, alongside any potential reuse of existing security services.

Reduced operational expenditure by consolidation of services: The building of shared security services reduces the complexity and diversity of the technical security products implemented by the organisation. Why manage five different firewall products when two or three would provide the diversity and security required? Why sustain three different identity directories and four different authentication mechanisms? Enterprise security architecture enables the identification of "champion" products – or, at least, reusable services – and the elimination of those products that provide little or no value to the organisation, reducing the overall cost of management of the security service. The identification and monitoring of relevant metrics can help to demonstrate the improved cost-effectiveness.

Increased agility of the business in reacting to new or increased threats as a result of new business strategies or requirements: A fully traceable enterprise security architecture provides organisations with excellent situational awareness, including a comprehensive understanding of the true threats, vulnerabilities and risks to which they are exposed and the controls that have been implemented to manage those risks. This understanding enables businesses to consider new approaches to IT delivery (or the delivery of new IT services) in full knowledge of the real risks, impact and cost that they currently face. The upsurge in the adoption of Cloud Computing has been dampened by security fears. The enterprise security approach enables these fears to be countered through a reasoned, business-focused approach to risk management.

This chapter has introduced some fundamental concepts regarding security architecture. The next chapter takes these concepts and begins to apply them to the security of Cloud Computing.

CHAPTER 7: APPLICATION OF SECURITY ARCHITECTURE TO CLOUD COMPUTING

Chapter 6 introduced some fundamental concepts of security architecture. In this chapter, we begin to apply some of these concepts to the area of Cloud Computing. The use of a security architecture methodology allows organisations to approach Cloud-based deliveries with the confidence that their security concerns have been identified and appropriately managed. Rather than acting as a blocker, security can act as a mechanism for enabling organisations to take advantage of the undoubted benefits of Cloud Computing.

Security reference model

I shall use a security reference model that I have used elsewhere to act as a framework for the discussion of approaches to securing Cloud services. This security reference model (SRM) is shown in *Figure 7*.

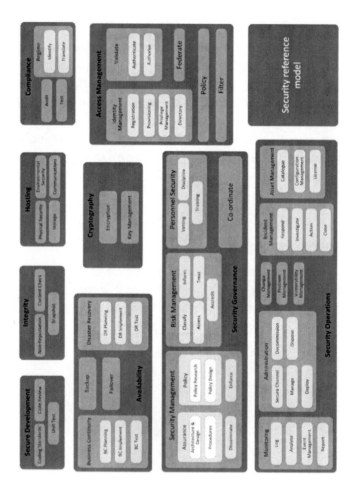

Figure 7: Presenting a Conceptual Security Reference Model

Using the terminology defined in *Chapter 6*, the SRM shown in *Figure 7* is a collection of conceptual security services. The SRM is based upon a framework I derived for a real system, but has been extended and modified, so as to provide a more comprehensive generic set of services. Now, there are some existing reference architectures with regard to Cloud Computing – notably those provided by NIST[43] and by the Cloud Security Alliance (CSA)[44]. However, as worthwhile and well written as these existing models are, they are not sufficiently granular for the purposes of this book. In addition to the architecture provided in their guidance document, the CSA have also issued their Trusted Cloud Initiative architecture[45], which is more granular in nature. However, from a personal perspective, I believe that this has jumped straight to the Logical level, and so loses some of the flexibility provided by working at the Conceptual level, making tracing back to underlying business requirements more problematic.

The original iteration of the security services within the SRM was derived from the examination of a set of organisational, legislative, regulatory and other requirements, together with the output from a business-focused risk assessment and guidance from a set of agreed security principles. The requirements were grouped together using areas of commonality (e.g. requirements relating to auditing) to form a series of conceptual services. The output of the risk assessment exercise was used to

---

[43] NIST Cloud Computing Reference Architecture, *www.nist.gov/customcf/get_pdf.cfm?pub_id=909505*.
[44] See Domain 1 of the Security Guidance for Critical Areas of Focus in Cloud Computing V3.0, *http://www.cloudsecurityalliance.org/research/security-guidance/*.
[45] *https://cloudsecurityalliance.org/wp-content/uploads/2011/11/TCI-Reference-Architecture-1.1.pdf*.

validate the set of conceptual services, i.e. to determine if the set of services provided an appropriate set of security barriers to mitigate the identified risks. Alterations were made to the services where they were not thought to be sufficient to mitigate the identified risks. This led to a set of conceptual services that the relevant business stakeholders were able to accept as being sufficient to meet both their business requirements and their non-functional requirements arising from the risk assessment. Now, this original set of services did not include all aspects of application security within its scope, and so the SRM has been through a number of iterations to make it more generic. The SRM now acts as a useful tool for sanity checking that the most common aspects of information assurance have been catered for in any particular design. It must be noted that not all services will be relevant to all applications – the purpose of the SRM is to help its users ensure that there is adequate coverage of those areas that are within scope.

For the rest of this book, we will be using the SRM to examine potential technical and/or procedural mechanisms for delivering the conceptual services it defines in the context of an application to be delivered using Cloud services.

Security service descriptions

Figure 7 provides a useful representation of a set of conceptual security services, but the SRM would undoubtedly be more useful with a description of what each of the security services are there to provide. These descriptions are provided in *Table 1*.

Table 1: Describing the services presented within the SRM

Service name	Level	Service description
Secure Development	0	Responsible for delivery of a secure codebase for the Cloud-based application.
Coding Standards	1	Responsible for providing developers with the guidance needed to produce secure code.
Code Review	1	Responsible for peer review of the code produced by developers against the Coding Standards.
Unit Test	1	Responsible for active code testing of modules before incorporation into the main branch.
Integrity	0	Responsible for ensuring that the application runs with integrity.
Non-Repudiation	1	Responsible for ensuring that actions can be attributed to those performing the action (the system, process or individual).
Content Check	1	Responsible for ensuring that the information being processed, stored or transmitted does not contain malicious content.

Snapshot	1	Responsible for providing snapshots of known good configurations (operating system, application, etc.)
Hosting	0	Responsible for ensuing that the physical infrastructure and operating processing hosting the Cloud application are secure.
Physical Security	1	Responsible for ensuring that the physical infrastructure is in a physically secure environment.
Environmental Security	1	Responsible for ensuring that the physical infrastructure is in a physical environment suitable for IT equipment.
Storage	1	Responsible for providing data storage facilities.
Communications	• 1	Responsible for providing voice and data communications facilities.
Compliance	0	Responsible for ensuring that the Cloud application meets the legislative, regulatory and internal policy requirements.
Audit	1	Responsible for assurance that the application is designed, built, operated and decommissioned in line with organisational standards.

Test	1	Responsible for delivering security testing requirements to ensure that the application does not contain known, or easily discoverable, vulnerabilities.
Regime	1	Responsible for defining the compliance regime that the application must deliver against.
Identify	2	Responsible for identifying the legislative, regulatory and internal policy requirements.
Translate	2	Responsible for translating the compliance requirements into the context of the application.
Availability	0	Responsible for ensuring that the application is available when required.
Business Continuity (BC)	1	Responsible for ensuring that the business functions provided by the application can continue in the event of the application itself not being available.
BC Planning	2	Responsible for designing the mechanisms needed to provide adequate levels of necessary business services in the event of a BC invocation.
BC Implement	2	Responsible for delivery of the requirements of the BC plan.

BC Test	2	Responsible for testing that the BC plan is effective.
Backup	1	Responsible for ensuring that suitable information back-ups are available.
Failover	1	Responsible for ensuring that services failover (securely) to an alternative, if required.
Disaster Recovery (DR)	1	Responsible for ensuring that IT services can be brought back online in a reasonable timescale after a disaster.
DR Planning	2	Responsible for designing the mechanisms needed to bring back agreed levels of IT service (RPO) within an agreed time frame (RTO).
DR Implement	2	Responsible for delivery of the requirements of the DR plan.
DR Test	2	Responsible for testing that the DR plan is effective.
Cryptography	0	Responsible for delivery of any cryptographic services needed to operate or manage the application.
Encryption	1	Responsible for delivery of Encryption services.

Key Management	1	Responsible for ensuring that encryption keys are appropriately managed.
Access Management	0	Responsible for ensuring that only authorised access to data and resources is permitted.
Identity Management	1	Responsible for ensuring that identities are managed securely.
Registration	2	Responsible for ensuring that identities are only created upon appropriate presentation of valid, authorised, credentials.
Provisioning	2	Responsible for the creation (and status amendment) of identities and associated credentials.
Privilege Management	2	Responsible for ensuring that identities can be assigned the privileges necessary for their function.
Directory	2	Responsible for storing identity and privilege information.
Validate	1	Responsible for checking that access requests are valid.
Authenticate	2	Responsible for checking that the presented credentials match those associated with the claimed identity.

Authorise	2	Responsible for checking whether the authenticated identity is authorised to perform the requested action.
Federate	1	Responsible for the trust infrastructures between federated identity partners.
Policy (AM)	1	Responsible for providing the policy information required for the other Identity Management services to operate.
Filter	1	Responsible for enforcing the access control decisions provided by the Validate services.
Security Governance	0	Responsible for providing an appropriate governance framework and associated standards.
Security Management	1	Responsible for providing appropriate security management capabilities.
Assurance	2	Responsible for ensuring that services are designed in line with organisational security standards.
Architecture & Design	3	Responsible for providing architecture and design security assurance.

Procedures	3	Responsible for providing security assurance of operating procedures.
Policy (SM)	2	Responsible for production of organisational security policies.
Policy Research	3	Responsible for incorporation of latest compliance/technology/business developments into policy.
Policy Design	3	Responsible for production of organisational security policies.
Disseminate	2	Responsible for dissemination of organisational security policies.
Enforce	2	Responsible for providing the organisational functions to enforce the provisions of the security policies.
Risk Management	1	Responsible for ensuring services are designed, built, operated and decommissioned in line with the relevant risk appetite.
Classify	2	Ensures that information assets are classified according to organisational policies.
Inform	2	Responsible for involving all relevant stakeholders in risk management.

Assess	2	Responsible for assessment of the risks associated with the service in scope.
Treat	2	Responsible for development of the approaches to manage each identified risk.
Accredit	2	Responsible for judging whether a system can be accredited for operation.
Personnel Security	1	Responsible for managing the risk that staff may present undue risk to the security of the service or data.
Vetting	2	Responsible for validating the identity and reference of a candidate. Includes conducting any other pre-employment checks in line with policy (e.g. criminal record and financial checks).
Discipline	2	Responsible for disciplining any breaches of security policy.
Training	2	Responsible for providing employees with the training necessary to fulfil their duties in a secure manner.
Co-ordinate	1	Responsible for co-ordination of the security services within the architecture.

Security Operations	0	Responsible for secure operation of the service.
Monitoring	1	Responsible for monitoring of the output, and performance, of the security services.
Log	2	Responsible for the logging of pre-defined security event information.
Analyse	2	Responsible for analysis of the logged security information – to highlight potential security incidents, for example.
Event Management	2	Responsible for management of events (e.g. to ignore, escalate or report).
Report	2	Responsible for production of regular reports or other exports of information from the monitoring service.
Administration	1	Responsible for secure system administration.
Secure Channel	2	Responsible for secure transit of management traffic.
Decommission	2	Responsible for secure de-commissioning of services.
Manage	2	Responsible for system administration.

Dispose	2	Responsible for secure disposal of hardware.
Deploy	2	Responsible for secure deployment of services.
Change Management	1	Provides security input into the change management process.
Problem Management	1	Provides security input into the problem management process.
Vulnerability Management	1	Responsible for the active identification and management of security vulnerabilities.
Incident Management	1	Responsible for the management of security incidents.
Respond	2	Responsible for formation of the initial response team.
Investigate	2	Responsible for investigation of the security incident.
Action	2	Responsible for deciding, and then enacting, the appropriate course of action.
Close	2	Responsible for closure of the security incident, including documentation of any lessons learned.
Asset Management	1	Responsible for management of the IT assets associated with the service.

Catalogue	2	Documents the IT assets associated with the service.
Configuration Management	2	Provides a managed approach to the recording of IT asset configuration.
License	2	Responsible for ensuring that all IT services are appropriately licensed.

Table 1 describes each of the different services included within the SRM. The "Level" column simply refers to a level of granularity; lower-level services can be grouped together to provide the higher-level services. For example, in order to provide a Secure Development service, it is necessary to consider such aspects as Coding Standards, Code Review and Unit Test services. As stated previously, the SRM is a generic model; experienced security architects are likely to offer different approaches for the delivery of the top-level services, based on their own experiences and expertise. The SRM is a useful tool; however, I am not positioning it as the holy grail of information assurance!

Service levels and contracts

In our discussions on the SRM so far, there has been no real indication of how the services interact to form a cohesive security solution. Furthermore, there has been no description of how the generic conceptual services can be moulded to provide solutions that are appropriate to a specific purpose or situation. I use a service-oriented approach to architecture, whereby the security services are as de-coupled as possible. This means that each service can be altered without affecting the operation of those services reliant on them – provided that the interfaces presented to other services remain commonly understood. In order to make a security service useable, the service must provide an interface that consuming services can access. The mechanism for defining the operation of each of the security services is that of a service contract, as described within the Open Group TOGAF9 methodology. A template service contract (based on that provided by Section 22.10 of TOGAF Version 9) is shown in *Table 2*.

Table 2: An example template for service contracts (adapted from TOGAF9)

Attribute type	Attribute	Description
General	Reference	Unique identifier of the contract.
General	Name	Descriptive name of the relevant service.
General	Description	Description of the service concerned.
General	Source	Origin of the contract artefact, e.g. a document or requirement.

General	Owner	Owner of the artefact – the individual governance body that provides authoritative validation of the details of the contract.
General	Version	Version of the contract.
• Business	• RACI	• Lists those who are responsible, accountable, consulted or informed, with respect to the operation of the contract.
• Business	• Functional requirements	• Specific set of bulleted items, listing exactly what activities the service performs.
Business	Importance to the process	Description of the criticality of this service to the business (should use a common set of criteria and criticality definitions).
Business	Quality of the information required	Description of the data quality requirements with regard to the information objects input into the service and the data quality requirements of the data output by the service.
Business	Contract control requirements	How the contract will be monitored and controlled (e.g. to ensure that it remains aligned to changing business requirements).

Business	Quality of service	Defines allowable failure rate for the service.
Business	Service level agreement	Defines the service levels expected of the service.
Non-functional	Throughput	Defines the throughput that the service must be able to process (e.g. volume of transactions).
Non-functional	Throughout period	Defines the period of time that the expected throughput will occur within (e.g. yearly, monthly, daily, hourly, etc.)
Non-functional	Growth	Defines the rate of expected growth in usage of the service (for a defined period – e.g. 10% over 12 months).
Non-functional	Service times	The times during which the service must be operational – e.g. office hours (9am – 5pm, for example).
Non-functional	Peak profile short-term	Description of peak usage on a short-term basis (e.g. 9 – 10am each day).
Non-functional	Peak Profile long-term	Description of peak usage on a long-term basis (e.g. month end, annual events, etc.)
Technical	Invocation	Description of how the service can be invoked (e.g. service end-points for technical services).

Technical	Invocation pre-conditions	Description of the conditions that must be met in order to invoke the service (e.g. authentication requirements).
Technical	Information objects	Describes the information objects that can be passed to the service for processing, and the information objects output by the service.
Technical	Behaviours	Criteria and conditions for successful operation, including dependencies. Lists any likely child services invoked in order to fulfil the purpose.

It can be seen from *Table 2* that service contracts can be used to define the activities that the service conducts, the information objects it consumes and the information objects it creates. Furthermore, it can be seen that the service levels and non-functional requirements are defined by the service contract. This is where the services can be customised to match each deployment situation; a service requiring 24-hour operation with zero downtime will likely require a different technical implementation from one with more relaxed requirements, for example.

Service contracts are incredibly important when defining any form of IT architecture, including security architecture. Service contracts define the levels of service provided by each security service. These service levels will often dictate the set of technical solutions that can be used to deliver each security solution. More importantly, these service levels will often enable a security architect to discount candidate security solutions that simply cannot deliver the required service levels.

I will not talk much more about service contracts in this book. Service contracts must be tailored to meet the specific needs of your application, and, as this book provides generic guidance, it does not make sense to provide a set of service contracts for each security service. Defining a set of appropriate service contracts is one of the critical tasks for your security architect.

Service models and the security reference model

So far, we have talked a lot about the SRM, but we have yet to discuss its relevance in the context of Cloud Computing. The remainder of this chapter uses the SRM to describe some of the differences inherent in the Cloud service models. Firstly, we will take a hypothetical application that an organisation is looking to host using Cloud services. The actual nature of the application is irrelevant – it simply needs to be an application that could be hosted using IaaS, PaaS or SaaS models. We will then discuss how the primary delivery responsibility for each of the security services within the SRM varies across the service models.

Infrastructure as a Service

Figure 8 illustrates the security responsibilities of the consumer and provider when an application is hosted upon an IaaS Cloud. *Appendix A* lists each of the SRM security services and provides a rationale for the assignment of primary delivery responsibility per service model.

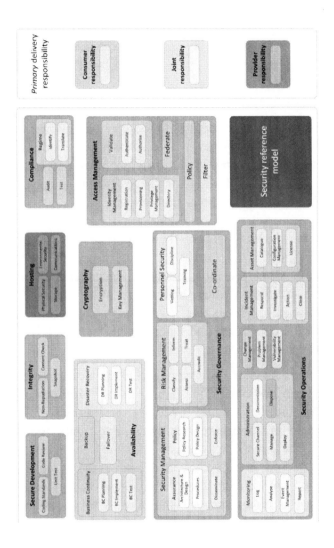

Figure 8: Illustrating the *primary* delivery responsibility for application security services when deploying on an IaaS Cloud

Figure 8 is quite clear in showing that the consumer retains primary responsibility for the delivery of the vast majority of the security services within the SRM, when deploying onto an IaaS Cloud. As should be expected, the Cloud provider has primary responsibility for those elements of service delivery relating to the physical hosting environment.

There are a number of services for which the delivery responsibility is split between both the service provider and consumer. The Filter service is a good example of one with joint delivery responsibility; the provider must implement technical controls to filter network access to the underlying Cloud infrastructure, whereas the consumer is responsible for implementing appropriate filter components within their virtual network and within their application. From a security perspective, the areas of joint responsibility are those where issues are most likely to occur. In the filter example, it is vital to ensure that all areas where a Filter service is required have been catered for by either the provider or the consumer, and that no gaps have been left in the overall security posture.

Availability is another SRM service that is an example of joint delivery responsibility. The service provider will typically provide contracted levels of service availability, perhaps including transparent failover across data centres. However, the consumer must still be cognisant of availability requirements over and above the contracted requirements, and ensure that the application can deliver these enhanced requirements. This may involve designing in the ability to failover from one Cloud service to another in the event of a major incident at the main Cloud provider.

Platform as a Service

Figure 9 shows a much more complicated scenario, where Platform as a Service is considered.

Given the nature of common PaaS services, it should be expected that the vast majority of security services must be delivered jointly by the provider and the consumer. In this example, we are assuming that the PaaS provides a set of security APIs for the purposes of authentication and authorisation, e.g. the Azure Access Control Services. This explains why the primary delivery responsibility for the Validate services within the Access Management service grouping of the SRM is assigned to the provider. The consumer must call such security APIs correctly, but the coding and maintenance of these APIs are the responsibility of the provider. Consumers of PaaS services should, therefore, look to PaaS providers that can demonstrate the adoption of a secure development life cycle.

Given what I said earlier about the areas of joint responsibility being the areas of most concern from a security perspective, it should not surprise you that I view PaaS as the hardest of the service models to secure. After all, almost all of the security services must be delivered jointly, and the interfaces and hand-off points between provider and consumer defined and controlled.

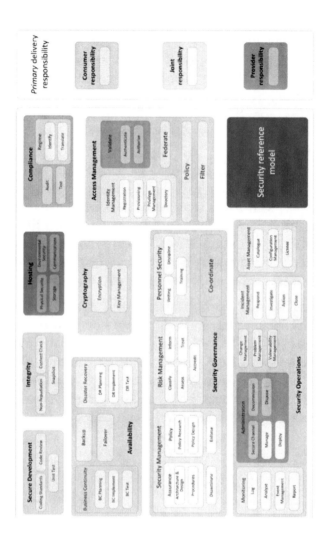

Figure 9: Illustrating the primary delivery responsibility for application security services when deploying on a PaaS Cloud

Even with the PaaS model, the consumer retains primary responsibility for a small number of services; most importantly, this includes the Compliance service grouping. Whilst the provider may claim to provide services in line with a set of requirements, such as PCI-DSS, the consumer would still suffer the consequences of any breach of compliance. It is, therefore, primarily the responsibility of the consumer to protect itself from breaches of compliance – regardless of the service model.

Software as a Service

Figure 10 shows the responsibility split for the final service model under consideration: Software as a Service.

With SaaS, many more of the security services are delivered by the provider. This includes the Secure Development services, as the application itself is here developed (or at least tailored and operated) by the provider. Your ideas about whether or not the fact that more services are delivered by the provider makes SaaS more secure than PaaS depend upon your level of trust in the provider. I would argue that it makes SaaS intrinsically easier to secure than PaaS, but that this does not necessarily make SaaS intrinsically more secure than PaaS.

There are some areas of joint responsibility, even with the SaaS model. For example, the Registration and Privilege Management services are both jointly delivered. The consumer must register their own users and must manage the privileges of their users within the application; however, both Registration and Privilege Management must be performed using capabilities delivered by the provider.

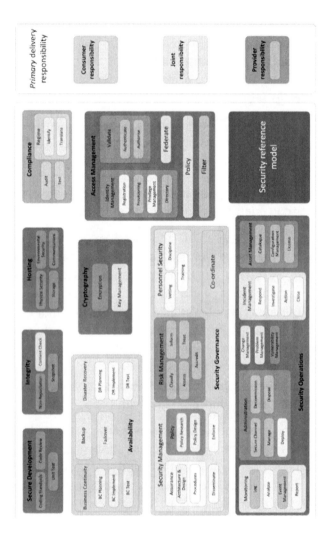

Figure 10: Illustrating the primary delivery responsibility for application security services when implementing a SaaS application

Conclusions

The aim of this chapter was to show how security architecture methodologies could be used to enable organisations to move towards Cloud Computing.

The discussion regarding the SRM has shown how security architecture can be used to identify potential areas of concern with the different service models – i.e. those areas where gaps may appear between the services delivered by the provider and those retained by the consumer.

In summary, the last two chapters have provided a high-level approach (based on architecture techniques) that can be used to define a set of technical and procedural requirements to appropriately secure a Cloud service:

- Derive and agree the business and non-functional requirements relating to security.
- Perform a risk assessment of the application.
- Identify any existing (or required) security principles.
- Identify a set of conceptual security services, derived from the requirements set, the risk assessment and the security principles.
- Draw up a series of service contracts relating to the identified services.
- Elaborate the conceptual services into a series of logical services.
- Determine appropriate technical and procedural controls to deliver the logical services, in line with the requirements of the service contracts.

This approach results in the production of a Cloud implementation that is demonstrably secured according to the needs of the business.

The next four chapters of this book delve into a little more detail in terms of the practical resources and mechanisms available to secure Cloud services. The services described within the SRM are explored for each of the service models, and example mechanisms for delivering these services are proposed.

CHAPTER 8: SECURITY AND THE CLOUD

This chapter begins with a brief overview of the existing guidance available to those with an interest in Cloud security. I then propose mechanisms for delivering the generic security services within the security reference model (SRM), i.e. those that are common to all three Cloud service models and where the delivery of the service is not overly impacted by the choice of IaaS, PaaS or SaaS.

Finally, this chapter also discusses the relative merits of the different Cloud deployment models from a security point of view.

Existing guidance

Cloud Computing has been billed as the next major advance in IT provisions for a number of years now – more than enough time for several different organisations to produce guidance in the area of Cloud security. The most established guidance document is arguably that produced by the Cloud Security Alliance (CSA)[46], a group composed of corporate and individual volunteers. The CSA document, "Security Guidance for Critical Areas of Focus in Cloud Computing" is in its third iteration at the time of writing, and now presents a relatively mature set of guidance across 14 different domains – from architecture through to incident response. The CSA guidance is a must-read

---

[46] *http://www.cloudsecurityalliance.org*. In the interests of transparency, I should note that I am a named contributor to versions 2 and 3 of the "Security Guidance for Critical Areas of Focus in Cloud Computing" document.

document, not least because it also represents a major element of the syllabus for the Certificate of Cloud Security Knowledge (CCSK) – the vendor-neutral Cloud security certification offered by the CSA. On the negative side, the guidance within the CSA document is almost completely focused on the Public Cloud model and, in places, is more theoretical than practical in nature. For example, a number of recommendations suggest that consumers should include their requirements in the contracts with their providers – contracts that are often non-negotiable. In addition to the security guidance document and the CCSK, the CSA also hosts a number of other initiatives relating to Cloud security, including:

- Cloud Controls Matrix (CCM)
- Consensus Assessments Initiative (CAI)
- CloudAudit
- CloudSIRT
- Telecom Working Group (TCI)
- Cloud Trust Protocol (CTP)
- GRC Stack (an integrated stack of four other CSA initiatives: CloudAudit, CCM, CAI and the CTP)
- Health Information Management (HIM)
- Cloud Data Governance (CDG)
- Security as a Service (SecaaS)
- Top Threats, and
- CSA Security, Trust and Assurance Registry (STAR).

Of these initiatives, I would particularly recommend that readers investigate the CCM and CAI; these documents are especially useful for those organisations looking to build

Cloud-based services (CCM) or procure them (CAI). The CSA STAR[47] initiative is one of the more recent CSA projects, going live in Q4 2011, but has the potential to also become one of the most valuable. The STAR Registry allows Cloud providers the opportunity to present the security services (using a CAI questionnaire) that are included within their offers. The Registry is sparsely populated at the time of writing, with entries only from Microsoft, Mimecast and Solutionary. The Registry is expected to become a valuable resource in the future for those looking to compare security services across vendors, and for those looking to demonstrate due diligence during their procurement processes.

The CCSK certification that I mentioned earlier tests the candidate's knowledge of the CSA security guidance document, together with their knowledge of the risk assessment document entitled, "Benefits, risks and recommendations for information security"[48], produced by the European Network and Information Security Agency (ENISA). This risk assessment document is only one of a number of interesting publications that ENISA have produced. Another ENISA document containing some worthwhile guidance is the "Security and Resilience in Governmental Clouds"[49] document, which includes a Strength, Weakness, Opportunity, Threat (SWOT) analysis with regard to the different deployment models, in a government context. The main landing page for ENISA's

---

[47] *http://www.cloudsecurityalliance.org/research/initiatives/star-registry/.*
[48] *www.enisa.europa.eu/act/rm/files/deliverables/cloud-computing-risk-assessment/at_download/fullReport.*
[49] *www.enisa.europa.eu/act/rm/emerging-and-future-risk/deliverables/security-and-resilience-in-governmental-clouds.*

work on Cloud can be found at *www.enisa.europa.eu/act/application-security/test*. I have made extensive use of the work of NIST within this document – primarily, their definitions of the Cloud service and delivery models. NIST also have a proud history in producing security guidelines, particularly in the area of operating system security. As you may expect then, given their work with Cloud Computing and security, NIST have produced their own special publication on the security of Cloud Computing: *Guidelines on Security and Privacy in Public Cloud Computing (Special Publication 800-144)*, 2011[50]. This provides a good overview of the security issues associated with the use of Public Cloud Computing services.

The final vendor-neutral organisation that I will mention here, in the context of generic advice, is the Open Group. There are a number of different Open Group working groups examining Cloud Computing, including a group working specifically on Cloud security. One of the first Open Group outputs in the area of Cloud security was the "Security Principles for Cloud and SOA" white paper, produced by the Cloud Computing workgroup[51]. This whitepaper presents a series of security principles, in the format recommended by TOGAF9, designed to guide the secure development of service-oriented architectures implemented in the Cloud. The security principles it describes are also often relevant to other forms of Cloud deployments. The Open Group is also home to the Jericho Forum® – an industry grouping "dedicated to advancing

---

[50] *www.nist.gov/customcf/get_pdf.cfm?pub_id=909494*.
[51] *www2.opengroup.org/ogsys/jsp/publications/PublicationDetails.jsp?publicationid=12511*.

secure business in a global open-network environment"[52]. Although not dedicated to Cloud Computing, the thinking advocated by the Jericho Forum® is particularly pertinent to delivery through Cloud services, and their output is usually thought provoking. The Jericho Forum® is the same group that produced the Cloud Cube model described in *Chapter 2.*

That concludes my brief round up of some of the existing guidance (and wider initiatives) with regard to the security of Cloud Computing. The next few pages provide some more detailed guidance on how a number of security services common to all service models may be implemented.

Common security services

In general, the security services defined within the security reference model (SRM) will be delivered differently for each service model. However, a number of the security services are technology-agnostic and so, therefore, are independent of Cloud service model. This section provides guidance on how these more procedural and/or organisational services may be provided.

Hosting

In the SRM, the Hosting service grouping is composed of the following services:

- Physical Security
- Environmental Security

---

[52] www.opengroup.org/jericho/.

- Storage
- Communications.

Regardless of service model, these Hosting services will always be delivered by the Cloud service provider (CSP).

Consumers should ensure that the physical security mechanisms employed by the CSP are sufficient to meet their requirements. This should not just be limited to the external perimeter security; consumers should ensure that the CSP data centres also include adequate internal security mechanisms, including internal access controls, internal security monitoring (CCTV, passive infra-red intruder detection systems, logging of access to sensitive security zones, etc.) and suitable procedures governing visitor access. In addition to the external and internal physical security of the building, consumers should also feel reassured that the CSP data centres are located in areas that are secure from multiple perspectives, including:

- Environmental threats (earthquakes, volcanic eruptions, flooding, severe weather, etc.)
- Civil unrest (Are the data centres located in stable political locations?)
- Government intrusion (Are the data centres located in countries where government access represents an acceptable threat?)
- Transport (flight paths)
- Resource availability (Is there a sufficient pool of skilled resources available?)

Some CSPs do not help themselves by keeping information regarding the location and physical security mechanisms of their sites out of the public domain. Consumers should be wary of CSPs that are unwilling to share such information, particularly if such information is still not available under non-disclosure agreements.

As with the physical security aspects, consumers should (where possible) ensure that they are content with the environmental controls implemented by the CSP. In the context of the SRM, environmental controls refer to those controls used to maintain a suitable environment for the IT equipment in terms of cooling, resilient and redundant power supplies and humidity controls. Those organisations with specific carbon reduction – or other "green" – targets, may also be interested in the efficiency ratings of the CSP data centres. Again, this information is not always available from the CSPs. However, a number of CSPs make the efficiency of their data centres a key point of pride and a selling point, e.g. Salesforce.com[53] and GoGrid[54].

Another key element of the Hosting service grouping, offered by CSPs of all description, relates to storage. Whether using IaaS, PaaS or SaaS, consumers are likely to need to store data within the CSP Cloud, and, therefore, within the CSP data centres. Whilst consumers may be able to secure their data via on-premise encryption (depending on the Cloud service), in other cases consumers will be reliant upon the storage security provided by the CSP. Where possible, consumers should feel comfortable with the mechanisms used by the CSP to secure their data when stored within the CSP Cloud. This should include examination of:

---

[53] *www.salesforce.com/company/sustainability/data_center_operations.jsp.*
[54] *www.gogrid.com/about/gogrid-facilities.php.*

- The access controls to the underlying storage systems
- The mechanisms separating data belonging to different consumers
- Support mechanisms for the storage (i.e. can customer data be taken off-site if storage failure requires investigation by the storage vendor?)
- The capabilities provided to consumers to remove their data from the CSP, and how such "deleted" data is managed by the CSP.

The final Hosting service within the SRM is the Communications service. Consumers should ensure that the CSP data centres have multiple communications links to ensure that their service remains available in the event of a network failure. As with the other hosting elements described in this section, such information is not always going to be available from the CSPs. In the event that such information is not available from their CSP, consumers must balance the risk of the service (or services) not meeting their requirements against the expected benefits of the Cloud service. Such a lack of information should not lead to the automatic disqualification of potential CSPs – that is, unless the consumer has specific critical requirements requiring absolute certainty of the mechanisms used to deliver those requirements.

Compliance

Compliance is, without doubt, perceived to be one of the major barriers to enterprise adoption of Cloud services. However, sufficient numbers of large organisations have adopted (or are adopting) Cloud services, which shows that the perceived compliance issues can be overcome – at least within the risk appetites of the organisations concerned. A good example of a large Cloud deployment by an organisation subject to a strict compliance is that of BBVA – a large Spanish bank, which is aiming to migrate 110,000 employees to Google Apps by the end of 2012[55].

Chapter 5 discussed some of the compliance issues associated with Cloud Computing, particularly with regard to data privacy and issues relating to compliance with the PCI-DSS.

Compliance is not a trivial subject to address, particularly for global enterprises. For example, the following link lists the data protection legislation of over 50 countries: *www.informationshield.com/intprivacylaws.html*. It is my view that compliance cannot be outsourced, which is why I have suggested, in *Figures 10, 11* and *12,* that compliance remains the primary delivery responsibility of the client, regardless of service model. I do not dispute that consumers may outsource delivery of services to providers offering compliant services. However, should the consumer or provider suffer a breach of compliance, the consumer would still suffer the consequences – such as loss of reputation and potential fines. The organisation always retains accountability for their own compliance and so, in my reference model, they also retain responsibility for ensuring that their services are delivered in a secure manner.

While a number of CSPs can legitimately claim to offer services that are compliant with standards, such as PCI-

---

[55] *http://press.bbva.com/latest-contents/press-releases/spain/bbva-banks-on-the-google-cloud(9882-22-101-c-92220).html.*

DSS (subject to very specific scopes), the consumer will still suffer the consequences if the systems that they build on such services become non-compliant. Such a situation could easily arise due to a misunderstanding of the scope of the compliance achieved by their CSP. Therefore, the risks of non-compliance remain with Cloud consumers.

Within the SRM, the Compliance service grouping is provided by the following services:

- Audit
- Test
- Regime
  - ○ Identify
  - ○ Translate.

So, how does this work in practice? Of these services, by far the most important – and hardest to deliver – is the Regime service. This is the service that is responsible for defining the compliance regime, and so sets the boundaries for the activities that are acceptable. In order to set the compliance regime, I suggest two different conceptual services: Identify and Translate. These two services perform two different – but equally critical – tasks, in terms of defining the compliance regime. The Identify service is responsible for the identification of all of the different compliance requirements (such requirements can be sourced from national legislation, industry regulation, organisational policies and other sources). I would recommend that the set of source requirements be validated by a qualified legal advisor to provide assurance that the set is defensibly comprehensive. Once a set of requirements has been identified, it is then necessary to place these requirements into context. For example, Principle 5 of the UK Data Protection Act 1998 states that,

Personal data processed for any purpose or purposes shall not be kept for longer than is necessary for that purpose or those purposes

But what does this mean in the context of your application? The purpose of the Translate service is to perform this trick of turning the typically generic language used in legislation and regulation into something relevant to the task at hand.

Now, you may be thinking that this all sounds like mountains of paperwork, which will severely impact upon the agility, flexibility and time to market that a move to Cloud is supposed to provide. At this point, I should highlight that I would not expect the Compliance service as a whole to need to be delivered by a Cloud project. ICT delivery projects rarely occur within an organisational vacuum; most organisations should already be aware of their compliance requirements, and so it's the Translate service that becomes critical. That is to say that the key task is to translate the existing – known – compliance requirements into testable requirements tailored for the Cloud-based service.

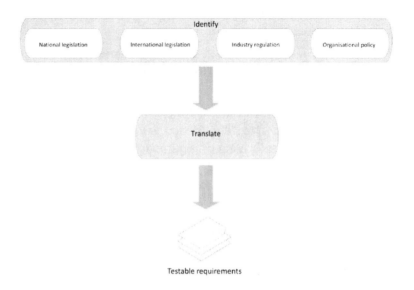

Identify
National legislation	International legislation	Industry regulation	Organisational policy

Translate

Testable requirements

Figure 11: Illustrating how the Identify and Translate services lead to a set of testable compliance requirements for an application

This process of generating a set of testable requirements is shown in *Figure 11*. Once you have a set of requirements, you can then test whether or not the Cloud services under consideration can meet those requirements. It is vital that the consumer pays close attention to the service levels promised by the provider alongside the liabilities and penalties for failure to meet these levels. There is little incentive (other than reputation management) for Cloud providers to meet strict service levels if their standard terms and conditions limit their liabilities for failing to meet them. Consumers should be wary of the advertised service levels and be comfortable with the possibility of the service levels not always being met. If you are comfortable with the likely actual service levels (and many reputable providers offer the facility to monitor their service level history), then you can go ahead and design your service with the comfort that your compliance requirements can be met.

Aside from the use of the SRM, there are some more straightforward, practical steps that enterprises can take to adhere to strict data protection rules. Possibly the most simple mechanism to ensure that your data does not leave the legal regime of your choice is to use a local Cloud supplier. For example, there are a number of Cloud suppliers within the UK that only operate data centres within the UK; such suppliers are, therefore, not going to place your data at risk of being transferred overseas (although there is no guarantee that IP packets between your on-premise systems and the Cloud provider will not be routed overseas). Similarly, a number of major systems integrators (e.g. Fujitsu, BT and Capgemini) also offer IaaS services that they claim are limited to the UK. An alternative route would be for the consumer to build their own Private Cloud and host this Cloud within the location of their choice. Of course, this latter option requires more initial investment and would not be suitable for those looking to take advantage of the pre-built services available from Public Cloud providers.

Security Governance

The Security Governance service grouping is one of the largest within the SRM, catering for:

- Security Management
- Risk Management, and
- Personnel Security.

There is also one more service included within the Security Governance grouping, and that is the Co-ordinate service. Whilst the primary responsibility for delivery of the services listed above may change, depending upon the chosen service model, the Co-ordinate service must always sit with the consumer (with the possible exception of when using a Cloud service broker). The purpose of the Co-ordinate service is to ensure that all of the other security services relevant to the application work together as a cohesive unit, regardless of who bears primary responsibility for delivery. I would, therefore, strongly recommend that consuming organisations assign responsibility for the co-ordination of security across on-premise and on-Cloud services to a named individual or team. This will help to maintain personal accountability and ensure that a close interest is maintained in the cohesiveness and effectiveness of the overall security architecture (for the Cloud and on-premise).

Cloud deployment models

The next few chapters of this book consider each of the Cloud service models in turn, and describe mechanisms for delivering the security services described within the SRM. However, these chapters do not consider the different Cloud deployment models. To fill this rather obvious gap, I'm going to use the remainder of this chapter to talk about the security characteristics of the different deployment models.

Public Cloud

Public Cloud is the deployment model most commonly associated with Cloud Computing. The security implications are very much encapsulated in its name: "Public". Public Cloud services are open to all: competing enterprises, individual users, malicious users and any other interested party. The Public Cloud model is shown in *Figure 12*.

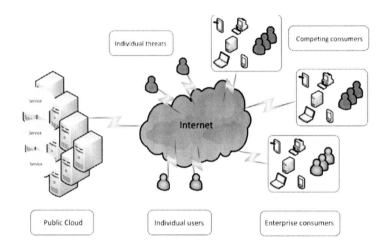

Figure 12: Illustrating the Public Cloud deployment model

All users have access to the shared resources.

The different customers of the Public Cloud service provider (CSP) are separated only by the mechanisms that have been implemented by the CSP; an insecure Cloud service could, effectively, bridge across its customer base. So, in the Public Cloud model, there are shared networks, hypervisors, access control services, storage and (depending on service model) shared platforms and applications.

A naïve consumer may have neglected to secure their communications to their "trusted" Cloud provider; it is vital that consumers realise that they are often connecting to their CSP over the untrusted Internet, and secure such connections appropriately. This book provides guidance on how to secure SaaS, PaaS and IaaS, and so I will not go into details here; the point of this section is to highlight the differences between the different deployment models.

Major Public Cloud providers are often global in nature, with data centres spread across the world, so as to provide resilience and redundancy and to deliver acceptable performance levels to local users. Such CSPs will often claim to be able to limit the transfer of data between these data centres, so as to enable their clients to meet compliance requirements relating to data location. However, there is often no cast-iron guarantee (e.g. acknowledgement of liability), should such CSPs accidentally allow data to leak from one data centre to another. This leads to a lack of confidence amongst potential consumers and helps to explain much of the concern that surveys often report with regard to compliance issues in the Cloud.

Of course, the Public Cloud model does have some security benefits to provide to their consumers. Firstly, the CSP has (likely) already heavily invested in security, particularly at the PaaS and SaaS level. This is an investment in property, technology, personnel and process that consumers can take advantage of and do not need to resource themselves. A second advantage of the Public Cloud model is the wide visibility of security incidents that these CSPs may have across their client base. There have been a number of anecdotal incidents where CSPs have noticed something amiss with their clients' activities – e.g. sudden increases in network traffic – and subsequently found that client services had been hacked and used to distribute illegal content. Such wide-ranging situational awareness can be a positive feature for many clients, particularly if the client does not have the staff or the contacts to be able to identify security threats currently active "in the wild".

In summary, consumers considering the Public Cloud model must be wary of compliance issues and be confident in the compensating mechanisms that they have adopted to protect themselves from other tenants accessing the service.

Private Cloud

The Private Cloud model is the diametrical opposite of the Public Cloud model. A Private Cloud is dedicated to the use of a single consumer. However, there is no requirement for the Private Cloud to be hosted and operated by the consumer. A Private Cloud can be outsourced to a traditional service provider, who may then operate the Cloud service from the premises of their client or from their own data centres. *Figure 13* outlines the Private Cloud model.

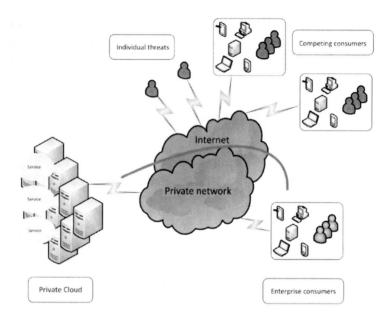

Figure 13: Illustrating the Private Cloud deployment model

The two networks indicate that Private Clouds may be accessed over Public or Private networks. The red line indicates that only authorised users may access the resources of the Private Cloud.

Figure 13 shows the two potential access mechanisms for a Private Cloud: the consumer's own WAN and, in the case of a hosted Cloud, perhaps the Internet. The red line within the diagram represents the barriers preventing the threat actors from accessing the Private Cloud. Unlike in the Public Cloud model, there is no multi-tenancy across different consumers. There may, however, be multi-tenancy implemented across different organisational units within the consumer. Indeed, this is where consumers may derive their cost-savings in their adoption of the Cloud model; different organisational units or services can now purchase compute or network resources from the Private Cloud, rather than having to invest in a multitude of discrete technology stacks.

From a security perspective, there is little doubt that the Private Cloud model offers consumers the most control. The consumer can dictate their own requirements and engage in detailed dialogue and negotiation with prospective CSPs. This is in direct contrast to the Public Cloud model, where it is often difficult (or impossible) for consumers to negotiate any deviation from the provider's standard terms and conditions or service levels. The flexibility offered by the Private Cloud model, therefore, enables consumers to implement the exact security solutions that they require, subject to the traditional constraints around cost! Consumers can also dictate the location of the infrastructure and, so, manage their own compliance risks.

The Private Cloud model is not without its issues, though. If the Private Cloud is only for one consumer – with their own set of particular security requirements – then the consumer will need to invest in the property, technology, personnel and processes needed to meet those requirements. If the consumer is planning to operate their own Private Cloud (rather than outsourcing its operation), then they must also accept the need to provide the necessary security resources.

The other main issue with Private Clouds, from a security perspective, relates to availability. Whereas Public Cloud services can present the illusion of infinite compute and storage resources, for Private Clouds, such an illusion is not sustainable. An organisation building a Private Cloud must still make provision for enough IT equipment to be able to cater for the maximum usage spikes; this will likely leave the organisation with the traditional issue of over-capacity, whereby resources sit idle, awaiting the next spike.

Hybrid Cloud

The Hybrid Cloud model applies to any combination of the other three deployment models. For example, a service delivered using both Private and Public Cloud resources would be described as a Hybrid Cloud. *Figure 14* outlines the different combinations of the other Cloud deployment models that can form a Hybrid Cloud.

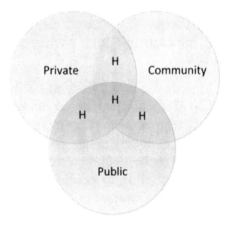

Figure 14: The Hybrid Cloud deployment

This refers to any combination of the Public, Private and Community Cloud models. These combinations are denoted with "H" in this diagram.

From *Figure 14,* it can be seen that there is at least one Hybrid Cloud configuration that does not involve Public Cloud services. This configuration would entail the use of Private Clouds in combination with Community Clouds. I point this out, as it is easy to forget that the hybrid approach does not necessitate the use of a Public Cloud.

Figure 15 uses a representation very similar to that used for the Private Cloud model within *Figure 13.*

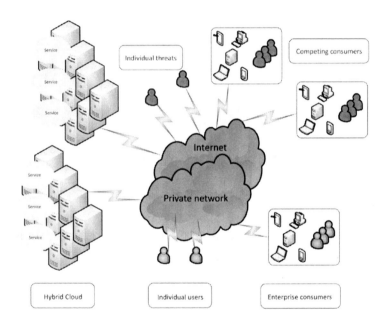

Figure 15: Illustrating a potential Hybrid Cloud deployment model (in this case a combination of Private and Public Clouds)

In *Figure 15*, the major difference from *Figure 13* is that I have removed the barrier between the Cloud resources and the threat actors. This brings me to the crux of the major problem I see with the Hybrid Cloud model. It is the worst of all worlds from a security perspective, especially when considering the combination of Private and Public Cloud models. Not only do consumers need to invest in all of the security resources associated with operating a Private (or Community) Cloud, but they must also implement the controls needed to operate in the Public Cloud. The Hybrid model is unsuitable for any organisation that has chosen to build a Private Cloud due to compliance issues that were deemed to be insurmountable using a Public Cloud model.

So, what reasons are there for an organisation to adopt the Hybrid Cloud model? Perhaps the primary driver relates to the over-capacity issue I touched upon when talking about the Private Cloud model. Rather than purchasing capacity that may only be used very rarely, an organisation may choose to maintain a presence on a Public Cloud service and "burst" to the Public Cloud for additional capacity when their Private Cloud becomes over-stretched. In this approach, an organisation's sensitive data remains within their Private Cloud – with only the occasional foray into the Public Cloud. Of course, from a compliance perspective, an occasional breach is still a breach. Another reason to adopt a Hybrid approach could arise when a consuming organisation is looking to adopt a "best of breed" approach. An organisation could, for example, want to make use of public SaaS services, but tie these together with some private IaaS services (e.g. storage).

From a security perspective, placing data into the Public Cloud immediately raises all of the issues associated with operating in the Public Cloud: multi-tenancy, data remanence (how does the Public Cloud provider manage data that has been deleted by the consumer?), and the potential leaking of data across geographic boundaries.

In terms of the security benefits that the Hybrid model offers over and above the Public Cloud model, there are none, in my opinion, with regard to Cloud bursting – other than the fact that private data is only placed at risk during the limited periods of time when the consumer is bursting to the Public Cloud. There may be some benefits to be gained from taking a Hybrid approach if the capabilities of the Public Cloud services can still be taken advantage of while sensitive data is retained within the more enclosed deployment model (i.e. in the Private Cloud).

Community Cloud

A Community Cloud sits somewhere between the Public and Private Cloud models. A Community Cloud caters for a closed community of organisations, typically bound by a common security and compliance regime. An excellent use case for a Community Cloud could include Government Clouds, or more niche areas, such as Cloud services aimed at law enforcement, health or education. *Figure 16* illustrates the Community Cloud model.

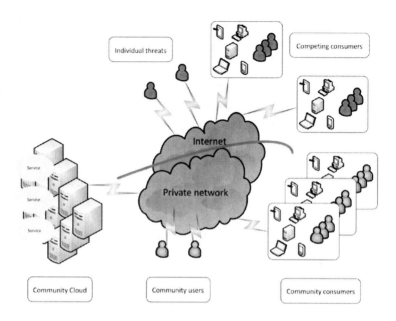

Figure 16: Illustrating the Community Cloud deployment model

As with the Private Cloud model, there are a series of barriers in a Community Cloud, which prevent access to the Cloud services for those outside of the authorised community. The Cloud services could be hosted within a commercial CSP data centre, within a data centre belonging to a member of the community, or perhaps within a shared data centre established by the community. The network links between the members of the community and the relevant data centres could be provided by a private network, or through use of the Internet.

The obvious advantage of Community Clouds over their Public Cloud equivalents is that the community gets to define their own shared security requirements and to dictate the location of the data centres. Another advantage of the Community Cloud model over the Public model is that it caters for a closed community, and so Joe Public (or Joe Competitor) will find it more difficult to compromise the service.

As the Community model sits between the Public and Private models, it, by definition, sits somewhere between those models in terms of the availability of capacity. Public Clouds present the illusion of infinite resources, and Private Clouds lead to either over- or under-provisioning; Community Clouds can help their users cater for usage spikes through the allocation of the resources not currently allocated to other members of the community. This is obviously based on the assumption that not all members of the community experience the same spikes in usage at the same times (which may not be as unlikely as it may sound, if talking about Community Clouds for the emergency services, for example).

One downside of the Community Cloud approach is the need for the members of the community to establish trust with each other, and also to agree to a common governance structure and approach with respect to their Community Cloud. Internal politics can be hard; politics within occasionally competing communities can be harder. A Community Cloud requires either a central or distributed governance body to define their requirements and to negotiate the terms, conditions and service levels expected of the CSP. This governance body must then procure the service, manage it once in operation, and, if necessary, continue managing it through to de-commissioning.

Overview of Cloud deployment models

Table 3 summarises the discussion about the merits of the different Cloud deployment models from a security perspective.

Table 3: Describing the relative strengths and weaknesses of the different Cloud deployment models

Deployment model	Strengths	Weaknesses	Candidate users
Public	• Provider security resources (personnel and technology) in place • Wide visibility of security incidents • Impression of infinite resources.	• Multi-tenancy • Compliance concerns.	• Small and Medium Enterprises (SMEs) and start-ups • Enterprises (primarily Test services, development services and stand-alone Internet-facing services).
Community	• Compliance service (Cloud service is designed to meet a common regime for the community) • Known (closed) community of users • Can be hosted by the community or outsourced.	• Requires a central body (or committee) to manage the service • Requirement to procure and implement the Cloud service • Requirement to trust other members of the community • Need to provide "community" security resources.	• Government • Other organisations with a shared security regime (e.g. industry groupings) • Academia.

Private	• Complete control by the consumer • Compliance • Closed set of users • Can be hosted by the consumer or outsourced.	• Need to invest in the initial implementation of the service • Requirement to provide their own security resources • Less ability to scale (burst) than either Public or Community Clouds.	• Financial services • Government departments and agencies • Enterprises with large existing investments in data centres and technology.
Hybrid	None	• Worst of both worlds: consumers need to secure their service both on-Cloud and on-premise. • Compliance concerns • Multi-tenancy.	SMEs and/or other organisations with low regulatory barriers.

In general, the amount of security control a customer has over a Cloud deployment decreases in the order shown below:

1. Private Cloud
2. Community Cloud
3. Hybrid Cloud
4. Public Cloud.

The only reason that I have placed the Hybrid Cloud model above the Public Cloud model is because (and you must remember this) Hybrid Clouds can be combinations of Private and Community Clouds, as well as combinations of Private and Public Clouds. As a principle, I would tend to argue that Hybrid Clouds should be viewed as being as secure as the most public aspect of the Cloud services concerned, e.g. a Hybrid Cloud of a Private and Public Cloud should be viewed as being as secure as the Public Cloud concerned.

CHAPTER 9: SECURITY AND INFRASTRUCTURE AS A SERVICE

In this chapter, I describe how the security services defined within the security reference model (SRM) – shown in *Figure 7* – can be delivered by those implementing an application upon an Infrastructure as a Service Cloud.

There are many IaaS providers offering a variety of different types of service. The Opencrowd Cloud taxonomy, found at *http://cloudtaxonomy.opencrowd.com/ taxonomy/infrastructure-as-a-service/* suggests the following categories of IaaS services:

- Backup and recovery
- Compute
- Content delivery networks
- Multi-Cloud management
- Services management, and
- Storage.

Personally, I would add Virtual Desktop Infrastructure (VDI) to this list. A number of Public Cloud providers offer VDI services, while the use of tools, such as those provided by Citrix and VMWare (e.g. VMWare View), are also common within Private Cloud environments. Admittedly, Citrix were offering VDI before the term "Cloud" became popular; however, VDI remains a valid use case for the Cloud model.

Examples of Public Cloud providers offering IaaS services include:

- Amazon (*http://aws.amazon.com/*)
- GoGrid (*www.gogrid.com*)
- Flexiscale (*www.flexiscale.com*)
- ElasticHosts (*www.elastichosts.com*), and
- Rackspace (*www.rackspace.com*).

Many traditional systems integrators also offer Cloud services, including IBM, BT, HP, Savvis, SunGard, CSC, Capgemini and Terremark.

Nirvanix (*www.nirvanix.com*) is a good example of an IaaS provider offering a specific infrastructure service; they offer Storage as a Service enabling enterprises, and others, to store their data in the Cloud.

In many ways, the task of securing IaaS services is extremely similar to that of securing traditional on-premise services. The prime differences are that the services are hosted by the Cloud service provider (CSP) and that the underlying networks, compute and storage resources are most likely shared with other consumers to a greater degree than they would be in traditional outsourcing models.

IaaS and the SRM

The rest of this chapter is dedicated to explaining how the services described within the SRM can be delivered when deploying services on an IaaS Cloud. Please remember that the SRM refers to the security services associated with an application to be hosted on a Cloud service; bear this in mind when you consider the scope of the following services discussed.

Secure Development

Within the SRM, the Secure Development services remain the primary responsibility of the consumer, as shown in *Figure 8*. After all, the CSP is only providing an infrastructure for the consumer to build upon.

Those building applications in the Cloud should, therefore, adhere to whatever best practices they have currently adopted for secure application development, albeit tailored to recognise some of the architectural differences. For example, if you are storing and retrieving data objects from shared storage, you may want to consider building in additional checks to ensure the data has not been tampered with since it was last accessed. Furthermore, you may wish to implement more stringent authentication of those making calls to any application programming interfaces that your Cloud-hosted service exposes. Such issues relating to architecture, integrity and access management will be described in the relevant sections of this book.

In terms of Coding Standards, Code Review and Unit Test services, there is little alteration required to the development processes used for more traditional developments (albeit that Cloud services can enable more efficient testing through their ability to spin up virtual test environments more easily than if using physical hardware). In addition, a number of testing providers also offer "testing as a service", whereby functional and performance testing can be configured and conducted using their Cloud-based services. Examples include *www.soasta.com/cloudtest* and *www.cloudassault.com*.

Integrity

In SRM terms, the Integrity service grouping is all about maintaining trust in the systems and data used to implement an application. The Non-Repudiation service is there to ensure that actions can be attributed to the correct individual, organisation or process – it, therefore, maintains trust in the provenance of the application or data. The Content Check service is there to ensure that the information object to be processed does not contain any nasty surprises, such as corruption, unauthorised modification or inclusion of malware. The Snapshot service is there to enable (almost) instant back-up to a known good image. The Snapshot service can also be used to capture the contents of a virtual machine image thought to be compromised, in order to perform a forensic analysis.

The Non-Repudiation service would typically be delivered using a combination of services defined elsewhere within the SRM. For example, Identity Management services would provide identity information, Monitoring services would provide event information and the Non-Repudiation services would provide the binding between the user and the event. The Non-Repudiation services could then make use of the Cryptographic services to provide true non-repudiation, or simply rely on the strength of the auditing if true, legally binding non-repudiation is not required. Why is Non-Repudiation an important service when building Cloud services? Consider the pay-as-you-go nature of Cloud services. You really want to be quite certain of who fired up the virtual servers for which you've just been billed. Consumers should, therefore, ensure that their providers offer appropriate audit trails, which indicate the users that have requested new or additional resources. Similarly, consumers should ensure that there is an adequate audit trail of the release of resources. This would ensure, for example, that the basic denial-of-service attack of simply shutting down a virtual infrastructure can also be captured in the audit trail.

The Content Check service grouping describes a vital collection of security capabilities. It encompasses traditional anti-virus mechanisms and file integrity mechanisms, together with higher-level mechanisms, to ensure that application-level traffic does not contain malicious content. In order to make this a little more real, consider the situation where our application in the Cloud processes significant amounts of XML-encoded data. How can you ensure that this XML-encoded data is safe to store and process, and does not, in fact, include any malicious embedded content or any entities containing SQL injection or cross-site scripting attacks? In the past, I have come across systems whereby attackers could supply XML that was stored in a back-end database, and then later passed from the database to a web browser. Stored cross-site scripting can be fun. But what is specific about Content Check and IaaS? Not an awful lot. In general, many of the best practices associated with traditional application deployments still apply:

- Don't trust user-supplied input.
- Don't trust information sourced from outside of your trusted domain.
- Don't assume that information has not been modified since it was created or last accessed.
- Don't allow code to run, unless you know what it's going to do.

Many of the tools used on a traditional deployment are, therefore, equally suitable for use on an IaaS deployment; your anti-virus system of choice, for example, can be used to protect your IaaS-hosted application (subject to licensing).

The move to Cloud is often associated with a move to more loosely coupled service-oriented applications and away from monolithic applications. This will typically involve exposing a number of service interfaces – each of which will (ideally) require some form of validation for the input passed to them. There are a number of security tools that can be used to perform such security validation/content checking, for example:

- Vordel (*www.vordel.com*)
- Layer 7 (*www.layer7tech.com*)
- Forum Systems (*www.forumsys.com*).

I should mention that such products typically call out to an external anti-virus engine to perform traditional checks for malware. These tools are necessary if you need to parse the XML being passed between your applications and your users to ensure that it does not include malicious content. If you can't parse the XML, you can't check the content. The requirements and risks underlying your security architecture will dictate whether such tools are necessary or whether you can rely upon the schema validation capabilities of more standard XML parsers.

One of the other drivers for an increased awareness of content checking within IaaS deployments is that the data to be stored and processed on your application is likely to be stored within shared storage systems. Depending on the level of trust you have in those shared storage mechanisms – and the level of risk that you are willing to accept – you may wish to perform some level of integrity checking prior to processing any information objects retrieved from such storage. The information objects in an IaaS environment will include virtual machine images; you really would not want to fire up a trojaned image.

Now, this is where the drivers underlying the Snapshot service become apparent. There is a need to capture a snapshot of an information object at a specific point in time and then be able to verify that the information object matches the snapshot when it is next accessed. The conceptual Snapshot service within the SRM would typically require the use of Cryptographic services to provide a signed hash of the information object in an actual implementation. There would also need to be technical services to generate the snapshot to validate the signed hash. Such services would reside within the Encryption conceptual service grouping of the SRM.

Availability

One of the perceived strengths of the Cloud model is the ability to deploy highly available systems without the need to invest in multiple data centres complete with fully replicated technology stacks, diverse communications links and data mirroring.

However, CSPs are not immune to availability issues themselves and, being high profile, outages of Cloud services – such as Office 365 and AWS EC2 – are well publicised. The Cloutage website (*www.cloutage.org*) tracks outages at Cloud service providers. The website has not been updated since May 2011 (at the time of writing), but the logged outages up until that time provide an indication of the numbers of outages across the Cloud landscape. The CloudSleuth[56] website (powered by Compuware) provides a view of the current availability and response times for a variety of Cloud providers.

In terms of maintaining the availability of a hosted service, you should consider whether your CSP has multiple data centres and whether these data centres are appropriately isolated from each other. If they have such facilities, then you could consider hosting your services across the CSP's data centres, in order to provide redundancy or resilience (or both) – depending upon your architecture. You should, however, bear in mind that any replication traffic between the two data centres would usually entail having to pay for the traffic to leave one Cloud and then enter the other. Most CSPs charge to transfer data into their Clouds and/or out of their Clouds, and, due to the levels of isolation, replication of data between data centres is usually viewed as two independent data transfers, and charged accordingly. Given that this is the case, consumers looking to implement their application using the IaaS model could, equally, look to host their services on two (or more) different IaaS platforms to provide their service with redundancy, rather than just using two data centres from the same provider. The pain of having to deal with two sets of management APIs could be mitigated through the use of tools that enable the management of multiple Clouds from a single interface, such as Rightscale® (*www.rightscale.com*). Consumers

---

[56] *www.cloudsleuth.net/web/guest/global-provider-view.*

could, therefore, move their workloads across Clouds more easily in the event of failure at their main provider.

Some Cloud providers build resilience – which can include geographic separation – in their offers. Amazon, for example, host separate instances of their services in different Regions, based on their geographical locations. Example Regions include US East, US West, the EU, Asia-Pacific and South America. Each Region is then split into separate Availability Zones. Availability Zones are designed to be insulated from failure within other Availability Zones. So, for example, if Amazon's Simple Storage Service® (Amazon S3®) should fail in one Availability Zone, clients using other Availability Zones in the same Region should not be affected. At least, that was the theory. Unfortunately, an incident in 2011 showed that the levels of isolation between Availability Zones were not sufficient to prevent an incident in one Availability Zone spilling over and affecting the wider Region. To their credit, Amazon provided an extensive review of the incident that led to this outage (essentially, it was a configuration management error during a scheduled upgrade, which rapidly snowballed into a major outage). This review can be found at *http://aws.amazon.com/message/65648*.

There's an interesting related blog entry from Don MacAskill of SmugMug (a customer of AWS) at *http://don.blogs.smugmug.com/2011/04/24/how-smugmug-survived-the-amazonpocalypse/*. This blog entry provides an interesting perspective on how the AWS outage referred to above looked to a customer who was able to keep their service running, and provides some insight into how they were able to stay up, whilst others were not.

I should point out that it's likely that Amazon have taken steps to resolve the process and technology issues that led to this outage. The use of Availability Zones should not, therefore, be discounted as an option providing a certain amount of resilience. For true resilience, however, consumers of AWS should consider running their service across different Regions, rather than relying upon Availability Zones. As noted earlier in this section, this solution would have cost implications, particularly if you need to transfer significant quantities of data between Regions. The following link provides further information on AWS Regions and Availability Zones: *http://docs.amazonwebservices.com/AWSEC2/latest/UserG uide/using-regions-availability-zones.html*.

Now, Amazon is not the only IaaS CSP capable of providing discrete Cloud services hosted within different data centres. GoGrid, for example, has two US data centres (in San Francisco and Ashburn), and one in the EU (Amsterdam). GoGrid also has a specific product (CloudLink) that provides their clients with a dedicated link between the two US data centres. CloudLink can be used to replicate traffic between the two data centres without traversing the Internet. Furthermore, CloudLink does not charge per data transfer over their service; there is, instead, a flat fee charged monthly, with the cost varying based on the bandwidth on the link. Details of the CloudLink service can be found at *www.gogrid.com/cloud-hosting/ cloudlink.php*.

ElasticHosts also offer services across different global availability zones; they have data centres in Portsmouth and Maidenhead (UK), in Los Angeles and San Antonio in the US, and a Canadian zone hosted in Toronto. According to

ElasticHosts   themselves   (*www.elastichosts.com/cloud-hosting/infrastructure*):

If you run your backup server in the same availability zone as the main server, you can transfer data between the two for free over a VLAN, but both would be affected by a catastrophic failure of the entire availability zone. On the other hand, you can survive such failures if you provision your backup server in another availability zone, but bandwidth between the two sites will be billable.

Regardless of the mechanisms that you decide are the most appropriate for your application – e.g. hosting across multiple CSP data centres, hosting across multiple CSPs or hosting across on-premise and the Cloud – you must still test that the failover mechanisms work as anticipated. There's very little worse than only finding out that your business continuity and disaster recovery plans are worthless at the time they are invoked. Better to test them regularly and fine-tune them such that, in the event of a serious incident, you are able to continue to serve your users.

As an aside, remember to adopt some of the traditional best practices around resilience and redundancy from the on-premise world, when designing your virtual infrastructure. Avoid single points of failure. Build in resilience where necessary. Design the infrastructure so that it can handle the failure of individual components gracefully. As with your Business Continuity and Disaster Recovery plans, test your infrastructure to ensure that failures are handled as expected.

Technical failure at a CSP data centre aside, the other major potential availability issue facing Cloud consumers is a commercial one. What happens if your CSP goes out of business? Or is acquired by a competitor, who then closes down the service? This is not an unprecedented situation; Coghead was a PaaS provider that closed down in 2009, with their intellectual property being acquired by SAP. Coghead customers had a matter of weeks to make alternative provisions for the operation of their services – a task made even more problematic by the fact that the services designed to run on the Coghead platform could not be easily ported to different platforms. Cloud consumers must ensure that the financial stability and potential for acquisition factors into their due diligence of prospective Cloud providers.

Cryptography

In terms of cryptography, IaaS consumers have the flexibility to build in (within reason) whatever levels of cryptographic protection they feel their application merits. This can be a benefit, or simply an extra development and/or implementation overhead, depending upon your perspective. PaaS providers may well offer their own cryptographic services within their platform. SaaS providers will either offer encryption or they will not; SaaS consumers have little room for manoeuvre. IaaS providers must develop and/or implement their own Encryption services (preferably using standard cryptographic libraries) for their hosted applications to consume. There is one important difference between on-premise and in-Cloud options when it comes to cryptographic services. Whereas it is possible to implement hardware security modules (HSMs) to generate and then store cryptographic keys securely on-premise, it is not possible for enterprises to install HSMs within a public IaaS environment. Of course, there is nothing to prevent the implementation of HSMs within a Private Cloud or even (potentially) within Community Clouds. A need to implement HSMs may also drive a requirement to use a Hybrid Cloud deployment model, whereby certain Encryption services (e.g. key generation) are provided on-premise and then consumed by applications hosted on the Cloud. This is an excellent example of the limitations of the Public Cloud model – there are certain classes of application (including those that require physical appliances) that just cannot be hosted on public IaaS Clouds.

Now, one of the major categories of IaaS provision is Storage as a Service. With Storage as a Service, consumers trust the CSPs with the secure storage of their data. Typical use cases for Storage as a Service include data storage for the purposes of archive, back-up and disaster recovery. More generic IaaS implementations will also typically require the use of persistent storage mechanisms – to store virtual machine images or as the back-end storage for database systems, for example. In both cases, if the consumer is sending sensitive data to the Cloud, then it is likely that this data will need to be encrypted – both in transit and at rest. Encryption in transit is fairly easily achieved; most CSPs will support the upload of data via SSL/TLS encrypted communications. This should be sufficient for most purposes. If it is not thought to be sufficient, then perhaps you should re-visit whether the use of Cloud in general is appropriate for the risks you believe you face. So, you can send your data into the Cloud relatively safely via SSL (always bearing in mind the increasingly shaky foundations of the trust infrastructure underlying the protocol). However, once the data has arrived in the Cloud, it is likely to be stored in the clear – i.e. in unencrypted form. Now, you could encrypt the data in a generic IaaS Cloud using key generation and the encryption algorithms implemented on one of your virtual servers. However, if your virtual server is compromised, then you have also likely provided the attacker with the mechanisms to access the encrypted data. If you're just using a Storage as a Service provider, then you will not actually have the option to implement your own encryption in the Cloud. You must either accept the storage of your data in the clear or, perhaps, make use of an Encryption service offered by the CSP. If you view CSP personnel as threat actors, then this latter solution is of little benefit – CSP staff could just as easily decrypt the data as encrypt it.

There is an approach that can enable you to store your sensitive data in the Cloud: on-premise encryption. If you perform your encryption on-premise, and only transfer the encrypted data, then you will never be sending your sensitive data out of your secure environment in the clear. This approach is suitable for archiving and off-site storage for back-up and disaster recovery use cases. It is less suitable for more transactional systems, with which you want to actually process the data once it is in the Cloud. In this instance, you are left with little choice but to encrypt and decrypt in the Cloud and accept the attendant risks (which vary across the different deployment models).

In summary, if you are performing encryption activities and view CSP staff as a threat actor, then perform as much of your data encryption (including key management) on-premise as you possibly can.

Access Management

The SRM includes a significant number of services relating to Access Management:

*   Identity Management:
    o   Registration
    o   Provisioning
    o   Privilege Management
    o   Directory.
*   Validate
    o   Authenticate
    o   Authorise.
*   Federate
*   Policy
*   Filter.

These services are shown in *Figure 17*, which is an extract from the SRM.

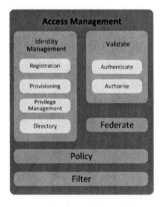

Figure 17: The Access Management service grouping of the SRM

The SRM is primarily there to guide us in the development of services relating to a hosted application; however, it would be remiss if we did not use the same conceptual services to secure the administration of the infrastructure hosting the application. I will, therefore, talk a little about the identity management services offered by some example IaaS providers, in addition to those relevant to hosted applications.

Identity Management

The Identity Management grouping includes the Registration, Provisioning, Privilege Management and Directory services.

The Identity Management services provide the underlying capabilities needed to facilitate the creation, amendment and deletion of users within your application, and to assign those users the appropriate privileges (whilst, at the same time, storing all of this information securely in a directory). Some of these services will be implemented outside of your organisation if you are following a federated approach to identity management. I will expand upon this more fully when I talk about the Federate service, later in this chapter. For now, just remember that your application needs users, that users will often need to be able to perform tasks according to their levels of authorisation, and that you need a mechanism to manage these users and tasks during the lifetime of your application.

How are such Identity Management services impacted by hosting an application within a public IaaS Cloud? The procedures governing registration are likely to be independent of whether an application is being hosted on-premise or in the Cloud. The requirements for the amount of proof a new user needs to provide to confirm their identity and then gain access your application will, typically, be driven by the compliance requirements. Registration requirements can vary from being practically non-existent (the provision of an e-mail address, for example), through more invasive information requests (name, address, date of birth, credit card details, etc.), to as strong a requirement as a physical inspection of official documentation, such as passports, to be conducted. Whilst the requirements regarding registration are independent from the delivery model, you must remember any compliance requirements dictating where you may store any personal data obtained during the registration procedure. This is particularly relevant if you are dealing with information relating to EU citizens or PCI-compliant data.

The Provisioning service relates to the creation, amendment and deletion of user accounts within the application, together with the mechanisms used to distribute credentials to the end-users. The Provisioning service can be viewed as the next step in the process of granting users access to your application necessary once you are content that the potential users have provided sufficient proof of their identify via the Registration service. How you provision users is very dependent upon your application and the underlying technologies that you choose to provide the Directory services (e.g. Windows® Active Directory® or Oracle Directory Services). I am not going to detail the processes for creating, amending and deleting users across these different products, as that's a level of detail too low for me to hope to cover in this book. However, I will comment upon the credential distribution aspect.

Clouds tend to be viewed as being quite insubstantial. You don't need your own physical data centre or physical hardware – rather, everything takes place in a virtualised environment in a CSP data centre. However, if your application requires strong authentication, it is highly likely that you will have to distribute physical tokens, such as those offered by RSA SecurID and Gemalto. These tokens tend to generate random sequences of numbers either upon request (usually after entry of a personal identification number), or at set intervals (e.g. every 60 seconds). These random sequences must then be entered as part of the process of authenticating to an application. This form of authentication represents the classic two-factor authentication model – i.e. it requires something you know (the PIN and the password associated with the account) and something you hold (the physical token generating the random number sequences). A consequence of implementing token-based authentication is that, even if the application itself is hosted in a CSP data centre, you must still have the facilities to store, configure and then distribute the tokens used to authenticate users to your application.

There is an alternative approach, however. There are a number of companies offering Authentication as a Service; CRYPTOCard (*www.cryptocard.com*), for example, offers a number of different authentication mechanisms, including token-based, SMS-token (whereby the random number sequence is sent to a mobile device via SMS) and simple password-based authentication. The authentication service provided by CRYPTOCard can then be integrated into your application using established protocols and standards, such as RADIUS and SAML. The obvious advantages of using an Authentication as a Service provider are that:

1. You no longer need to concern yourself with the problems of implementing your own Provisioning or Directory services for the application.
2. You no longer need to worry about storing, configuring and distributing physical access tokens.

The obvious disadvantage of using an Authentication as a Service provider is that you will have to entrust the task of controlling access to your application to a third party. The capability for trusting third parties is dependent on your organisational culture. The purpose of this book is to provide you with options for securing your Cloud applications; which option you should choose to adopt for your application depends upon your particular situation.

So, I've outlined some of the options available for the logical elaboration and physical implementation of the conceptual Identity Management services for a hosted application. But what options are available to provide Identity Management services at the IaaS level? There may be valid concerns that the effort expended to implement strong authentication for an application could be undermined by weak authentication to the hosting infrastructure.

I'll begin with Amazon Web Services. Amazon was one of the first movers in the IaaS arena, and this is reflected in the relative maturity of the Identity Management services available to their customers. For example, Amazon offers AWS Identity and Access Management (IAM). The AWS IAM service (*http://aws.amazon.com/iam/*) enables Amazon customers to provision multiple users, each with their own unique password, and to then define the AWS APIs and resources they can access. AWS IAM also enables customers to group their users according to their access needs, and to add conditional aspects to their access – e.g. by providing the option to restrict the times of day that users can access the services. AWS customers can, therefore, implement the established security control of segregation of duties; for example, they can have one group of users able to manage the virtual compute resources hosted upon AWS EC2, whilst another group of users is responsible for managing the Storage services hosted upon S3. (In reality, some users will likely require access to both EC2 and S3 in order to configure persistent storage for EC2 services.)

As well as AWS IAM, Amazon also offers the capability to implement two-factor authentication (2FA) via the AWS Multi-Factor Authentication service, AWS MFA (*http://aws.amazon.com/mfa/*). AWS MFA supports 2FA via either physical tokens – in the form of Gemalto hardware tokens – or via software installed onto a physical device, such as a smartphone or tablet that can also generate one-time passwords. This, effectively, makes the smartphone or tablet the equivalent of the physical token. Each user defined using AWS IAM can be allocated their own authentication token using AWS MFA.

Unfortunately, many other Cloud providers are not yet able to offer quite such comprehensive identity management capabilities. Rackspace, FlexiScale and ElasticHosts, for example, only allow for a single account owner, with no capability to add in other users at the top level. This approach limits the ability of their customers to segregate duties, and also makes the single account owner account a single point of failure. However, I should point out that Rackspace are major contributors to the OpenStack initiative (*http://openstack.org/* – an open source approach to building IaaS services), and that the OpenStack project does include role-based access control (RBAC). The OpenStack approach to RBAC is to segregate the virtualised resources into "projects". Projects consist of a separate VLAN, volumes, instances, images, keys, and users. Users can then be assigned privileges – such as Cloud Administrator, IT Security and Network Administrator – for individual projects. This is a flexible approach that enables users to have different roles for different projects. The following link provides further details of the OpenStack approach to identity and access management: *http://docs.openstack.org/trunk/openstack-compute/admin/content/users-and-projects.html.*

GoGrid also offers some basic RBAC capabilities. The GoGrid Portal enables multiple API keys (used to access the GoGrid management functions) to be generated per account. Different roles (limited to superusers, system users, billing users or read-only portal users) can be associated with each API key. This is explained further at *https://wiki.gogrid.com/wiki/index.php/API:Anatomy_of_a_GoGrid_API_Call#Security.*

This section has highlighted that, in terms of maturity, there is significant variation between the different Identity Management capabilities offered by public IaaS providers. On one hand, you have CSPs adopting a simple single-account model and, on the other hand, you have CSPs offering more fully featured capabilities. The level of capability on offer should factor into your choice of CSP.

Validate

The Validate service grouping is responsible for checking that a user's claim to be able to access a service is legitimate. The Validate service grouping contains two conceptual services: Authenticate and Authorise. The Authenticate service validates that the user credentials presented in an access request (e.g. a password or a token-generated number sequence) match the credentials associated with the user. The Authorise service validates that a user has been granted permission to access the resource (e.g. data, a system or a function) that they are attempting to access. So, authentication is focused on validating the user, whereas authorisation is focused on validating their access.

Authenticate

When it comes to the application that you are choosing to host on an IaaS service, you have free rein to decide upon the most appropriate authentication mechanism. Example mechanisms could include traditional username/password authentication, certificate-based authentication, token-based authentication, or the use of federated identity management techniques, such as OpenID®. I provide more detail about OpenID in the section covering the Federate service (*see page 167*).

However, from a security purist perspective, you could question the true merit of implementing an application-level authentication mechanism that is stronger than the authentication mechanism protecting the operating system and underlying infrastructure. If you have lost trust in the underlying infrastructure, then you can have little faith in the operating systems and applications it hosts.

Now, once you have configured your operating system, there is little to prevent you from implementing whatever strength of authentication you require in the operating system. However, you have less control over the authentication mechanisms to the CSP management portal or API used to create, shutdown, modify or administer your virtual services.

This being the case, you need to take a close look at the authentication mechanisms supported by the different IaaS providers. I mentioned that Amazon supports multi-factor authentication for users via their Multi-Factor Authentication service (*http://aws.amazon.com/mfa/*) in the section on identity management, earlier in this chapter. However, one AWS authentication issue that has been highlighted is the unfortunate tendency for AWS consumers to embed their security credentials within their Amazon Machine Images, particularly where that AMI includes processes that need to communicate with other AWS services. This can become a major issue if the consumer concerned decides to share that AMI, as other users making use of the shared AMI could choose to make use of the embedded credentials. Do not embed your AWS credentials within AMIs that you intend to share.

Unfortunately, support for multi-factor authentication to Cloud services is not widespread throughout the public IaaS ecosystem. RackSpace, for example, tends to rely upon the use of an API key to secure access to their management API, and a simple username and password for access to their management portal. An example of the XML encapsulating the information needed to authenticate to the RackSpace API is as follows:

```
<credentials
xmlns="http://docs.rackspaceCloud.com/auth/api/v1.1"
    username="hub_cap"
    key="a86850deb2742ec3cb41518e26aa2d89"/>57
```

In the RackSpace example, the username making the call is "hub_cap", and the API key – equivalent to a password – is shown in the key value. The security of the administrator access to the RackSpace IaaS is, therefore, tied to the security of the API key.

ElasticHosts are very similar to RackSpace in terms of the authentication mechanisms available to secure access to their administration functions. API calls to the ElasticHosts management services make use of HTTP Basic Authentication, with the user's Unique User ID (UUID) as the username and their API key as the password[58].

GoGrid adopt a very similar approach to both ElasticHosts and Rackspace, in terms of the need to use an API key. It may appear that ElasticHosts add an additional element of security by requiring that all API calls include an MD5 signature. The MD5 signature is a concatenation of the chosen API key, the user's shared secret (equivalent to a

---

[57] Taken from: *http://docs.rackspace.com/auth/api/v1.1/auth-client-devguide/content/ Request_Response_Types-d1e9.html*.

[58] *www.elastichosts.com/cloud-support/api#authentication*.

password) and a timestamp[59]. However, in effect, this does not improve upon the solutions of ElasticHosts or RackSpace. The GoGrid API key and shared secret combination is, effectively, just a simple username/password combination. The main difference between the GoGrid and RackSpace/ElasticHosts approaches is that GoGrid supports multiple users, and so multiple API keys are available. GoGrid recognises the problem of securing access solely by the confidentiality of API keys and associated shared secrets, and, on the GoGrid Wiki, presents the following guidance:

Keep track of your API Key and shared secret values and be sure to keep them confidential as they will allow you to make authorized API requests against your GoGrid account. If an outside party obtains access to your API Key or shared secret, they will be able to make API requests that could affect your servers.

Authorise

The Authorise service is responsible for authorising access to a resource. In the context of a hosted application, the Authorise service dictates the requirements for authorisation to data or functionality. In the context of the underlying IaaS, the Authorise service dictates the requirements for authorisation to add, delete or modify IaaS resources (compute, storage, etc.)

In order to perform authorisation, you would normally require:

- A set of resources to be protected

---

[59] *https://wiki.gogrid.com/wiki/index.php?title=API:Anatomy_of_a_GoGrid_API_Call&diff=5263&oldid=prev.*

- A set of authorised users, to whom access is to be granted
- A directory, in which details of users and their access privileges can be stored
- A policy to dictate who can access resources and the levels of access they have (e.g. Create, Read, Update, Delete permissions)
- A Filter service to enforce the policy.

I've used the Conceptual services from the SRM in the above bullet points. From a logical service perspective, you would expect to use more common industry terms associated with identity and access management – such as "Policy Information Points", "Policy Decision Points" and "Policy Enforcement Points".

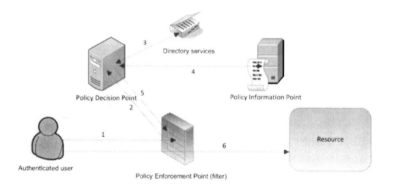

Figure 18: Illustrating a typical authorisation sequence

Figure 18 shows a typical authorisation sequence. The steps shown are as follows:

1. An authenticated user requests access to an information resource, and the request is intercepted by a Policy Enforcement Point (PEP).
2. The PEP queries a Policy Decision Point (PDP) on whether the access request is authorised.
3. The PDP queries a Directory service to obtain details of the authenticated user, e.g. concerning group membership, access privileges, etc.
4. The PDP queries a Policy Information Point (PIP) to request information on the access policy for the resource concerned (e.g. a list of groups allowed to access the resource, any time-based or IP-address constraints, etc.)
5. The PDP applies the policy based on the information it has obtained and informs the PEP of the access decision.
6. The PEP now allows the user to access the resource (or not, if the request has not been authorised).

From a technology perspective, the interactions described above would likely involve a number of different http(s) requests transporting SAML tokens backwards and forwards. I'm not going to go into further detail on the technologies providing authorisation capabilities; there are enough textbooks dedicated to identity and access management – I couldn't possibly do the topic justice in one short section. However, there is a Cloud-specific element to the authorisation process described in *Figure 18*. Whilst it is not necessary to host each of the PEP, PDP, PIP, etc. on separate servers, hosting certain functions on separate servers can provide Cloud consumers with additional flexibility. For example, if you have concerns about hosting the personal data contained within a directory on a Cloud server, then you could host the Directory service, Policy Information Point and Policy Decision Point on-premise. In this scenario, only the Policy Enforcement Point and the resource itself will be hosted within the Cloud – and the Cloud provider may not require knowledge of the sensitive personal data that you are keeping on-premise.

Similarly, you could host the Directory, PIP and PDP services on one Cloud, and then manage access to all your other Cloud services from this single (although, I would suggest, replicated) authorisation Cloud.

Another option for delivering authorisation services would be to adopt a federated approach, e.g. through the use of protocols, such as OAuth.

Federate

Federation has already been mentioned a number of times in this chapter – primarily in relation to authentication and authorisation – but without much detail as to what it means. Federated identity management is a trust-based approach to identity management, whereby an organisation trusts the authentication and/or authorisation decisions made by another organisation. Federation can be useful to prevent users constantly having to re-enter their credentials every time they begin to interact with a new service. Similarly, federation can be useful in enabling smoother interaction across services – one service may be provided access to information held by a separate service, for example.

When talking about federated authentication, two terms that commonly occur are "identity provider" (IdP) and "relying party" (RP). Relying parties are sometimes known as "service providers" (SPs). The relying party is the application or service to which a user is attempting to authenticate. If the service incorporates a federated authentication scheme, then, at this point, the RP will ask its identity provider whether or not the user is authenticated. If they are, the RP will then provide the user with access. If not, the user will typically be prompted to authenticate using the RP's own authentication mechanisms.

Federation can be used to deliver a number of benefits in addition to providing single sign-on across services. Consider the case of a Community Cloud hosting a shared application. One approach to delivering identity management for such an application would be to have a centralised directory containing accounts for each user from the community requiring access to the service. However, this approach has some negative implications:

- The community needs to find someone to administer this directory.
- The users will acquire yet another set of credentials to either remember or, in the case of a physical token, keep safe.
- Access management processes will be laborious, requiring authorisation from within the source organisation, and then actioning (possibly via another authorisation step) at the centre.

An alternative strategy would be to adopt a federated approach, whereby the shared application will trust the authentication decisions made at each of the organisations that comprise the community. So, the shared application becomes an RP, and each member of the community becomes an IdP. This approach has a number of advantages:

- Authentication decisions are made by each community organisation.
- There is no central user directory – each community organisation controls the user information it allows to leave its secure domain.
- Access management processes occur at a faster rate – accounts can be created at the IdP and then replicated to the RP – using SPML[60], for example.

Of course, there are some compromises associated with this approach – e.g. members of the community must trust that the other members implement appropriately strong authentication mechanisms. There can also be a degree of pain involved in the implementation of the cryptographic services needed to establish the technical trust between the different parties. Finally, significant effort needs to be expended to establish the governance structures needed to establish the trust infrastructure, i.e. to set appropriate standards for authentication. However, overall, I prefer this federated approach over the more centralised model, due to the greater flexibility it offers to the users and the ability of the community organisations to retain control of their own information.

---

[60] *www.oasis-open.org/committees/tc_home.php?wg_abbrev=provision.*

Two commonly implemented federation technologies in the Web space are OpenID[61] (which provides federated authentication) and OAuth[62] (which provides federated authorisation). You may well find that you already have an OpenID identity, without even realising it. Google, Yahoo, Facebook, PayPal and others are already making use of OpenID. As OpenID is a federated authentication protocol, it enables you to use an OpenID IdP to sign in to other services that have signed up to trust your OpenID IdP.

The following link provides guidance on how you can use Google as an OpenID IdP for your application (i.e. how you can enable users to log-in to your application with their Gmail credentials): *http://code.google.com/apis/accounts /docs/OpenID.html*.

The OpenID website (*http://openid.net/get-an-openid/*) provides links to other OpenID providers, should you prefer to use a provider other than Google.

Before implementing OpenID, you will need to make sure that the Registration and Authenticate services on offer through your OpenID provider of choice are inline with your requirements for these services. One of the advantages of the security architecture approach that I introduced earlier is that you should have service contracts for the Authenticate and Registration services that provide the relevant functional and non-functional requirements to inform your decision. If you are not content with the registration processes on offer at the OpenID IdP, then you

---

[61] *http://www.openid.net.*
[62] *http://oauth.net/.*

could consider adding additional registration checks for when users first access your application. You could also consider the use of a secondary authentication mechanism to supplement OpenID authentication, should you wish to avoid placing complete trust in OpenID.

OAuth is a complementary, but different, protocol from OpenID. OAuth is used to provide access to specific services within a wider application – for example, it allows another application to access your Facebook status updates, but does not provide that application with your Facebook password, or with access to other aspects of Facebook. As with OpenID, OAuth has been widely adopted by the major web companies; OAuth service providers include Facebook, Google, Yahoo and Microsoft, amongst others. As an example, *Figure 19* illustrates how Microsoft has adopted OAuth within their Live service.

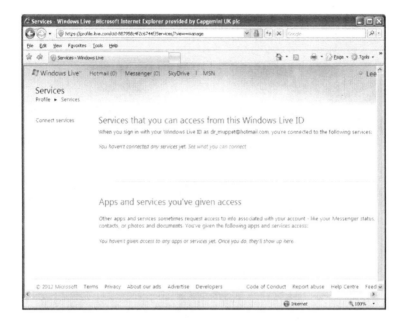

Figure 19: Illustrating the OAuth approach adopted by Microsoft

Figure 19 shows two aspects of the approach taken by Microsoft:

- The top half of the screen lists the services that you can access using your Live ID. I have not signed up to any services using this particular Live ID, and so this area is not populated.
- The bottom half of the screen lists the services that you have allowed to access aspects of your Live services (e.g. Messenger functions).

Figure 20 provides a good example of the other services with which Windows® Live can interact via OAuth.

Figure 20: Illustrating some other services with which Windows® Live could interact via OAuth

Once a user has decided that they would like to be able to use their Live credentials to access another service, they will be redirected to that other service and presented with a screen similar to that shown in *Figure 21*.

Figure 21: Illustrating the process of allowing a Live Messenger account to access LinkedIn

In *Figure 21*, I am being asked to allow my Windows® Live ID to access my LinkedIn account. It's interesting to note that I can limit the amount of time for which that access will persist.

I wrote earlier that OpenID and OAuth are complementary protocols. In practice, this means that an application provider can use OpenID to authenticate their users, but then use OAuth to limit the functionality available to such users – all without actually requiring access to the personal information or password associated with the OpenID account. OpenID can be used to share information with other services; however, the information to be shared is at the discretion of the user – a benefit for the users and, potentially, the application provider, if they are subject to privacy regulations.

Now, OpenID is probably the most widely implemented federated authentication solution, but it is not, however, the only solution.

In the earlier section on the Authenticate service, I mentioned CRYPTOCard. CRYPTOCard is able to act as an IdP through their support for the Security Assertion Markup Language (SAML)[63]. You can, therefore, implement multi-factor authentication – including the use of SMS soft tokens (i.e. authentication codes sent to your mobile phone) – using federation across all of your applications using a Cloud-based service. One weakness in this approach is the requirement to populate the CRYPTOCard Directory with your user details, which may cause difficulties in some tightly regulated environments. Please note that other providers offer services similar to those available from CRYPTOCard – e.g. CA[64]. Alternatively, you could implement a product like PingFederate[®65] to enable your own Cloud-based applications to support federated identity management. PingFederate supports OpenID, SAML and WS-Federation[66].

---

[63] *www.oasis-open.org/committees/tc_home.php?wg_abbrev=security*.
[64] *http://www.ca.com/us/two-factor-authentication.aspx*.
[65] *www.pingidentity.com/our-solutions/pingfederate.cfm*.
[66] *www.oasis-open.org/committees/tc_home.php?wg_abbrev=wsfed*.

Another, more common, use for federated identity management is to authenticate to Cloud-based services using an on-premise identity provider. In this scenario, the Cloud-based applications are the relying parties. This can enable Cloud consumers to make use of existing investments in authentication and identity management technologies. At the same time, such an approach also enables Cloud consumers to present their users with transparent access to services, whether they are hosted on-premise or on-Cloud. Furthermore, by hosting the identity provider on-premise, organisations effectively keep the keys to their Cloud-based applications and data within their secure domain (although this protection could be bypassed, should the underlying Cloud infrastructure suffer from a weakness lower down the technology stack – e.g. in the hypervisor). This approach to federated identity management is most common when implementing SaaS delivery models, particularly if the consumer makes use of multiple SaaS providers.

So far, I have written about how the Federate service may be implemented within an application that you may wish to host on an IaaS Cloud. Some IaaS providers also support federated identity management, such that you can manage your virtual infrastructures whilst authenticated via federation. Amazon allows you to create temporary security credentials that you can then distribute to users that have been authenticated via your existing authentication service. Once your users are in possession of these temporary security credentials, they can then access the AWS Management Console directly, without being prompted for a password. The lifetime of the temporary security credentials are defined at the time of creation. The following link describes how to create temporary security credentials using the Amazon Security Token Service (STS): *http://docs.amazonwebservices.com/IAM/latest/ UsingSTS/Welcome.html*.

Once you have understood the nature of AWS temporary security credentials (and also the AWS services that support such credentials), you can then consider using this approach to secure access to the AWS Management Console, as described in the following link: *http://docs.amazonwebservices.com/IAM/latest/UsingSTS/S TSMgmtConsole.html*.

As Amazon themselves note, just because security credentials are temporary does not mean that the actions of those with such credentials will not be permanent. For example, should a user with temporary credentials start a new Amazon Machine Image, this virtual server will continue to run (and be charged) even after the temporary credentials of the user have expired.

Policy

The Policy service (within the Access Management grouping) of the SRM is responsible for setting the policy for access management decisions. Policies are required to dictate which users (individuals, application accounts, service accounts, etc.) are allowed access to an information resource (data, function, server, etc.), and what privileges they are allowed to that resource (e.g. Create, Read, Update, Delete, etc.) Policy Information Points (and their role in the authorisation process) were mentioned during the section on authorisation. At the Logical and Physical levels, policy may be stored centrally on a PIP, however, in many cases, policies will be physically implemented at a more local level. For example, firewall policies are more than likely (and recommended) to be stored separately from access management policies at the application level.

There is little more to be said about policy in this context – your policies for access to information resources must be dictated by your business requirements. The business requirements must indicate which types of users require access to which information resources, and at what level this access should be granted.

The Policy service interacts with a number of other SRM services – notably the Authenticate, Authorise and Filter services – to perform many of the tasks commonly associated with information security (e.g. preventing unauthorised access to information, or, in a positive light, enabling authorised access to information).

Filter

The Filter service within the SRM serves as a good illustration of what is meant by a conceptual service. The Filter service enforces the Policy requirements. As it's a conceptual service, it does not dictate how filters should be delivered at the Logical or Physical level. Why is it a good illustration? Because the Filter service tells you what you need to do (deny or allow access), but does not tell you how to do it, or how to enforce it. Although it may not look it at first sight, this is a good thing. Consider the many different areas where you need to control access, for example:

• Data centre
• Storage

- Data
- Operating system
- Database
- Application
- Network
- Hypervisor.

Each of these aspects will require its own physical set of filtering technologies. At the lowest level, data centres will require suitable mechanisms to prevent unauthorised access to the equipment that they host. With a Public Cloud, this is an issue for the CSP, while with Community and Private Clouds this issue may be one for the Cloud consumer. Similarly, physical and administrative access to the low-level storage devices is typically within the purview of the CSP in the context of a Public Cloud.

When you get to the data level – i.e. the definition of which users (including applications) are allowed access to specific data items – things start to become more complicated. For example, Amazon offers a number of different Storage services, including the Simple Storage Service (S3) and Elastic Block Storage (EBS). Access to data stored within the AWS S3 storage can be secured in a number of ways, as highlighted at: *http://docs.amazonwebservices.com/ AmazonS3/latest/dev/UsingAuthAccess.html?r=6105*.

In summary, access can be controlled at an S3 bucket level or at an object level basis, and the controls can be applied in a number of ways to enable sharing either just within your AWS account or across different AWS accounts. The key point here is that the enforcement point is still within the realm of the CSP – AWS, in this case. It should also be noted that the decision on which form of access control technology should be adopted sits within the Policy service.

However, at the EBS level, consumers can format the EBS volumes and mount them, much as normal disk devices. GoGrid, Flexiscale and others offer similar functionality to provide storage facilities for their virtual services. The point is that once the drives have been mounted, it is down to the CSP consumer to decide which users can access the device (via Policy), but then enforce that access control (via Filter) within the operating system. At this point, the enforcement of access to the mounted volume is the responsibility of the consumer, but the responsibility for ensuring that only the consumer (or those with whom the consumer has shared access) can access the storage volume itself sits with the CSP.

But you also require logical and physical Filter services at levels other than just the data. What about the network? The majority of the network access controls in the IaaS environment are provided by the CSP. The CSP infrastructure is directly connected to the Internet; it is the responsibility of the CSP to ensure that Internet-based attackers cannot compromise the underlying infrastructure. They must (and mostly do) implement appropriate firewalling and intrusion prevention technologies. However, what about your virtual servers? Once you have your Cloud server instance, you are commonly placed directly onto the Internet. If you do not have a host-based firewall, then you are at the mercy of whatever network-based controls the CSP may have implemented. From an AWS EC2 perspective, this is a relatively safe position to be in, as the AWS firewall capability offered as part of the standard AWS service adopts a default deny position, i.e. all network traffic to the instance will be dropped. This means that it is the responsibility of the consumer to open up access to the network ports required to run their service. Once again, this is really a policy question, with the filter aspect being implemented by AWS. However, with other CSPs, you may find that firewalling is an optional extra (e.g. with ElasticHosts – as shown at *www.elastichosts.com/cloud-support/tutorials/firewall*). GoGrid have yet another approach to implementing Filter services at the network level: they enable their customers to rent physical hardware firewalls[67]. Given that GoGrid also offers the possibility of renting dedicated physical servers sitting on the same networks as their multi-tenant Cloud servers, this approach provides their consumers with great flexibility regarding the amount of multi-tenancy that they are comfortable accepting. But, even so, whilst the Policy setting may be the responsibility of the consumer, the actual implementation of the filter is the responsibility of the CSP.

Once you reach the level of the operating system, the responsibility for implementation of Filter services sits firmly with the consumer. Consumers can implement host-based firewalls, host-based intrusion prevention systems, operating system ACLs on file system objects and any other traditional operating system-level access control mechanism. Given that the servers are operating within the Cloud, it is worth considering what controls are available over and above those that would be installed in an on-premise environment. For example, a tool such as CohesiveFT's VNS-Cubed®(VNS3™)[68] gives you the potential to implement your own virtual Private Cloud VNS-Cubed enables a Cloud consumer to implement an

---

[67] *https://wiki.gogrid.com/wiki/index.php/Hardware_Firewalls.*
[68] *http://www.cohesiveft.com/products/vns3.*

SSL-encrypted overlay network that effectively prevents CSP staff from being able to access or view the consumer's data whilst it is within the encrypted overlay. CSP staff would still have the ability to close down instances, should they wish, and to see data entering and leaving the overlay – be that to and from the Internet or to and from the underlying storage devices. However, they would not have access to the traffic flowing across the overlay network itself. Such tools can be useful filters with regard to CSP staff, who are, otherwise, fairly impervious to the controls available to Cloud consumers (Vyatta[69] offers a similar network overlay solution, but one which also includes stateful firewalling, intrusion prevention and other security capabilities). Another example of a product aimed at IaaS Clouds, and virtualised environments in general, is Catbird® (*www2.catbird.com/*). Catbird offers a number of different security capabilities, but, in the context of the Filter service, the most relevant capability is that for controlling inter-virtual machine traffic. In a Private Cloud environment, Catbird can also be used to control which virtual machines can be hosted on a single physical server, providing a useful tool for ensuring that compliance boundaries can be maintained in a virtualised environment.

Going back slightly towards the network level, Amazon offer a service that enables their consumers to make use of their virtualised (and multi-tenant, unless using Dedicated Instances) services, but without having these virtual servers being routable from the Internet. This is their Virtual Private Cloud (Amazon VPC) service[70]. In order to connect to a VPC, consumers must set up an encrypted Virtual

---

[69] *www.vyatta.com/solutions/cloud*.
[70] *http://aws.amazon.com/vpc/*.

Private Network (VPN) connection to AWS. The VPC service enables consumers to effectively extend their data centre into the Amazon Public Cloud, as no other AWS consumers can access the VPC and the VPC is not directly routable[71] from the Internet. Amazon also offers another service for consumers looking to avoid the Internet completely: Amazon Direct Connect[72]. Direct Connect provides a direct connection between the consumer premises and an AWS Direct Connect location without using the Internet as the transport mechanism. However, consumers making use of these AWS services are reliant upon the filter controls implemented by AWS to separate the VPC service from the rest of the Amazon Public Cloud.

At the application level, you can consider using a Web Application Firewall (WAF) to provide a filter if you are using an IaaS Cloud to host a web service. There is little difference here between applications hosted on-premise and those hosted within a Cloud; at the application level the WAF is there to filter out malicious traffic lurking within the http(s) communications. It may be worth noting that there are some Web Application Firewalls that are aimed specifically at the AWS EC2 market – e.g. those from Imperva and Riverbed's Stingray product (formerly known as Zeus).

One of the issues to bear in mind when considering the logical elaboration, and subsequent physical implementation, of the conceptual Filter service is that any such controls must be appropriate to the task at hand. Consider a traditional firewall. Most firewalls are very good

---

[71] AWS consumers can configure an Internet Gateway to enable routing between a VPC and the Internet.
[72] *https://aws.amazon.com/directconnect*.

at controlling the network communications that traverse them – dictating allowed sources, the allowed destinations, the allowed types of traffic between the sources and destinations and, often, ensuring that the traffic adheres to the relevant protocol specifications. But this is often insufficient for today's complex applications. Consider a web application processing XML-encoded information transported via SSL/TLS encrypted communications. A traditional firewall will be blind to the nature of the traffic flowing over the encrypted channel; even if it could see the XML on the network, it most likely would not be able to parse the XML so as to understand whether the traffic was malicious. A more appropriate choice for a Filter service would be an XML firewall specifically designed to be able to parse XML and perform basic checks – such as schema validation – but also spot more elaborate attacks, such as embedded malicious binaries. XML firewalls are particularly relevant where a Cloud consumer is building a web services-based information system. I mentioned a number of such XML firewalls products in the section on the Integrity service earlier in this chapter, namely:

* Vordel (*www.vordel.com*)
* Layer 7 (*www.layer7tech.com*)
* Forum Systems (*www.forumsys.com*).

The Layer 7 SecureSpan® XML gateway is available as an Amazon Machine Image ready for use on EC2[73]. It is worth noting, at this stage, that there are a wide variety of security applications available as pre-packaged AMIs. A registry of different Cloud solutions (including those offering AMIs

---

[73] *https://aws.amazon.com/solution-providers/isv/layer7tech.*

and others) can be found at
https://aws.amazon.com/solution-providers.

A similar registry is available for solution providers
working with GoGrid, such as Dome9 and CohesiveFT, at
http://exchange.gogrid.com/.

At the database level, consumers should consider the
specific use of database security products. Such products
are able to understand the queries and commands being
passed back and forth between the database server,
application servers and administrators. The database
firewall (also known as database activity monitoring)
market is now fairly mature, with many of the early market
leaders now having been acquired by more established
entities – for example:

- Guardium (purchased by IBM: *www-01.ibm.com/
  software/data/guardium/*)
- Secerno (purchased by Oracle: *www.oracle.com/us/
  products/database/security/index.html*)
- Sentrigo (purchased by McAfee: *www.mcafee.com/us/
  products/database-security/index.aspx*).

Where you have a need to monitor the activities of your
database administrators, or you wish to lock down the
database access available to application accounts, then you
should be looking towards database activity monitoring
products as part of your Filter service.

One of the major differences between a physical
deployment and a virtual deployment is the addition of a
new attack surface: the hypervisor. In a Public Cloud
environment, the security of the hypervisor is firmly within
the realm of the CSP. In a Private or Community Cloud, the

consumer is in the position to be able to specify the security controls protecting the hypervisor and controlling the inter virtual machine traffic flowing across it. In a VMWare environment, there are a number of different options for providing this capability, e.g:

- VMWare vShield® Zones (*www.vmware.com/products/ vshield-zones/overview.html*)
- Cisco Virtual Security Gateway (VSG) (*www.cisco.com/en/US/products/ps11208/index.html*)
- Catbird® (*www2.catbird.com/our_services/trustzones.php*)
- Trend Micro Deep Security® (*www.trendmicro.co.uk/products/deep-security/index .html*)
- HyTrust® (*www.hytrust.com*).

Understandably, the VMWare vShield product only works with VMWare hypervisors, and the Cisco VSG requires the use of the Cisco Nexus® 1000 virtual switch. However, there are situations where either product could be used (e.g. when implementing a Cisco UCS® infrastructure). The other products (Catbird, Deep Security and HyTrust) all offer the most comprehensive support for VMWare-based environments. Deep Security, for example, makes use of the VMWare vSafe APIs to provide agentless security capabilities within VMWare environments. Those organisations using Xen® or Hyper-V hypervisors and looking to implement Deep Security would be limited to an agent-based solution offering only the anti-malware capabilities.

In essence, many of these products sit beside the hypervisor (monitoring and controlling the traffic flows between the hosted virtual machines), and can also be used to control the network to and from the hypervisor (protecting the hypervisor itself). These products typically allow you to group virtual machines into zones and then control the network traffic between these zones (although they also work on an individual virtual machine basis). This approach allows you to mimic a more traditional n-tier architecture[74] by using different zones, rather than different physically separate network segments. Concerns have been raised by some – including the UK Government National Technical Authority for information assurance (CESG) – that little assurance should be placed in these products. The primary reason for such concerns relates to the fact that compromise of the hypervisor itself would render these controls worthless; they could be bypassed through re-configuration at the hypervisor level. As such, CESG and others would not recommend that these tools be used to provide a security barrier between domains at different levels of trust, but rather that they may be used within a security domain. Another valid concern is that whilst, with a traditional n-tier architecture, you may consider implementing different firewall products at the different tiers, with a virtualised environment you will be limited to the one product – be that vShield, Catbird, or whatever product you have implemented. *Figures 25* and *26* illustrate the differences between a traditional n-tier application architecture and a virtualised alternative, making use of a hypervisor-based firewall.

---

[74] For example, a service where presentation, application and data services are separated using firewalls (*see Figure 22).*

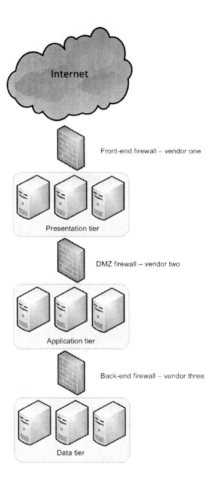

Figure 22: A traditional n-tier security approach

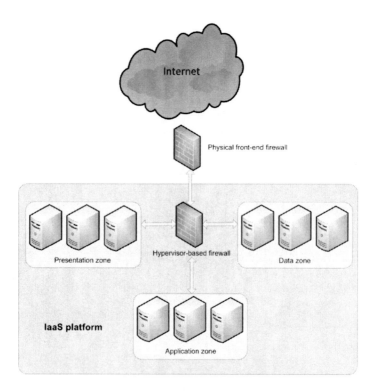

Figure 23: Implementing an n-tier architecture on an IaaS platform using zones

You can see from *Figure 22* that the traditional approach makes use of three different firewall products (so as to guard against failure of a single product), and has the ability to control traffic across each tier boundary. *Figure 23* shows that, instead of physically separate firewalls and servers, we now have a set of virtualised servers grouped into different zones, with the separation (filter) being provided by hypervisor-based firewalls.

My advice is that you consider your levels of risk and act accordingly; do you believe that the assets within your virtual environment are valuable enough to merit an attacker "giving away" a valuable zero-day (i.e. unpublished) hypervisor exploit? If so, then you need to invest in suitable levels of physical separation within your application (e.g. implement a physically separate de-militarised zone). If not, then you may be willing to rely upon the Filter services that hypervisor-based technologies can deliver.

Security Governance

With the IaaS service model, the primary delivery responsibility for Security Governance remains with the Cloud consumer. The Cloud consumer retains primary delivery responsibility for the Security Management, Risk Management and Co-ordinate services. The Personnel Security service is a joint delivery responsibility, reflecting the fact that CSP staff have access to the infrastructure, whilst consumer personnel have access to the virtualised environment. The Security Governance services from the SRM are shown in *Figure 24.*

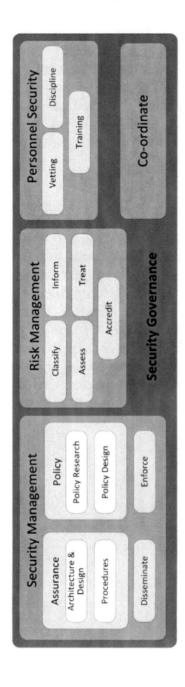

Figure 24: The Security Governance service grouping from the SRM

Security Management

The Security Management service delivers (conceptually) many of the traditional functions of an IT security practice:

* Setting Policy
* Disseminating Policy
* Enforcing Policy
* Assuring Policy implementation within technical design and operational procedures.

The Policy service within the SRM has two aspects; Policy Research and Policy Design. The Policy Research service provides the capability to research latest developments with regard to compliance, technology and evolving business requirements related to the application to be hosted upon an IaaS Cloud. The output from the Policy Research capability can then be passed to the Policy Design service, which outputs security policies relevant to the application. Policy Design is likely to be something of an iterative process. For example, an initial security policy may help to dictate which IaaS providers are suitable to host your application, perhaps based on their geographical locations. The next iteration of the application security policy may then incorporate some specific aspects relating to the CSP – for example, those individual offerings of the CSP that are approved for implementation, those that are not judged to be suitable, etc. These security policies can then be used to drive more technical policies, such as those required for access management purposes, personnel security vetting, encryption standards, etc.

Unfortunately, one of the areas where information security often fails is in the transition from information security policy through to actual implementation. The SRM includes two services in relation to this: one aimed at ensuring that all relevant individuals are aware of the policy requirements (Disseminate), and the other at ensuring that the policy requirements are enforced (Enforce). Dissemination can be achieved via security awareness training (for consumer personnel) and via the provision of appropriate guidance documentation. The goal of the Disseminate function is to ensure that everyone understands their security obligations and – just as importantly – to convince them that following the policy is in their own best interests. The Enforce capability is necessary to shepherd those elements of the organisation (or user community) that may not buy into the message that is promulgated via the Disseminate service. The Enforce capability must have appropriate links to Personnel functions, in particular the Discipline service, to ensure that adequate and proportional sanctions are in place for those that may choose not to adhere to policy. The Enforce function also requires explicit support from authoritative figures within the consumer organisation, to provide policy implementation with the necessary impetus.

The final capability provided by the Security Management service grouping is that of Assurance. From a security management perspective, Assurance is about assuring that the requirements of the relevant security policies have been adopted within the technical design of the application and the associated operating procedures. Wider security assurance testing activities are covered elsewhere (e.g. in Compliance and Vulnerability Management). The Assurance capabilities require sufficient consumer expertise in the Cloud technologies in question in order to be effective. The staff involved must be able to understand whether or not a proposed technical architecture meets the policy requirements. A lack of understanding will likely lead to failures in meeting policy requirements, and so increase the possibility of a security or compliance breach. Whilst I am of the view that the development of Cloud Computing is an evolution, rather than a revolution, the security impacts of this evolution on underlying technical delivery, service-oriented design and global compliance requirements are significant. Organisations should consider the training requirements of any existing assurance function. An "old-school" security assurance function could derail any number of Cloud deployments, due to misunderstandings of the underlying technologies or an overly risk-averse approach. The cost of training and up-skilling of security personnel should be outweighed by the benefits of enabling a risk-managed (rather than risk-averse) approach to adopting Cloud services.

Risk Management

I don't intend to write reams of text describing the Risk Management service grouping. Most organisations should have adopted a preferred approach to risk management, and there is little reason why most such approaches should not be extended to the Cloud. At a high level, a risk management approach should consist of the following steps:

- **Classify:** Classify your assets in terms of their value to the business. Value could be measured in terms of confidentiality, integrity and availability, for example. Value could also be measured in monetary terms.

- **Inform:** Involve the relevant organisation personnel. Asset owners should be involved in assessing and agreeing the classifications associated with their assets. Suitable safeguards should be built into the process to ensure that the human tendency to overvalue their own assets is adequately managed (e.g. by involving higher levels of management with sight across the assets concerned).

- **Assess:** Assess the threats (competitors, hackers, governments, employees, CSP staff, journalists, etc.) to your assets. Be realistic. Assess the attack surface of your application. Consider which potential vulnerabilities could realistically be exploited by each threat. Consider the business impacts of a vulnerability being exploited by a threat actor. Bear in mind that the business impact may be dependent upon the threat actor concerned. For example, a well-meaning customer may identify a potential vulnerability in your application and inform you through a published notification process. A black-hat hacker may identify the same vulnerability and post an exploit on the Internet; the same asset, the same vulnerability – but the impact is different because of the actions of the threat actor. Document your risks (e.g. in terms of assets, vulnerabilities, threats and impacts) in an accessible manner. There are a number of published risk analysis methodologies, such as FAIR[75] and OCTAVE[76].

- **Treat:** Using the risk register produced by the Assess service, treat each risk appropriately and in turn. Standard treatments would include accept, transfer,

---

[75] www.cxoware.com/what-is-fair.
[76] www.cert.org/octave.

mitigate or avoid. It is perfectly acceptable to simply accept risks that fall within the tolerance of your organisation. Not every risk must be mitigated or avoided. Document the proposed treatment of each risk in a risk treatment plan, ensuring that any mitigations are explained to a level of detail sufficient to allow the overall risk owner to judge the suitability of the mitigation.

- **Accredit:** An appropriate figure within the organisation should review the risk analysis and associated risk treatment plan, and confirm that they are content that all relevant risks have been identified and appropriately treated. This final sign-off effectively provides a security accreditation for the application. Some organisations may wish to extend this process, such that formal accreditation is only offered after penetration testing has been completed and the necessary remediation undertaken.

Personnel Security

Within the SRM, I have marked Personnel Security as being a joint delivery responsibility when considering the IaaS service model. This reflects the fact that CSPs must hire, manage and release staff in a manner that does not place the security of their customers' data or service at undue risk. By the same token, IaaS consumers must also ensure that their users, application developers, system administrators, database administrators, etc. are also appropriately managed.

I suggested three main services within the SRM; Vetting, Discipline and Training.

Vetting: The Vetting service (in combination with Compliance and other services via associated service contracts) dictates the levels of background checking needed prior to employing personnel or moving personnel from a less sensitive role to a more sensitive role. The UK Centre for the Protection of National Infrastructure offers some useful guidance on pre-employment checks at *www.cpni.gov.uk/advice/personnel-security1/screening*.

Background checks can vary in intrusiveness, from simple identity verification through to extensive interviews with acquaintances of the individual concerned, together with financial and criminal record checks. From a consumer perspective, Vetting processes for their users accessing Cloud-based resources should be no different to those used elsewhere within their organisation. Consumers must, however, content themselves that the Vetting processes adopted by the IaaS providers match the levels of rigour that they themselves require, or else accept a known residual risk.

Discipline: The Discipline service ensures that appropriate sanctions can be enforced against users and/or employees who fail to meet their security obligations. As with the Vetting process, consumers should simply adopt their existing disciplinary processes when implementing services in the Cloud.

Personnel Security: The final Personnel Security service within the SRM relates to Training. As noted earlier in this chapter, it is vital that your users receive appropriate training, so that best use can be made of the new ways of working offered by Cloud Computing. This is as true for security professionals as it is for other IT professionals. Developers should receive training on the implications of working with the chosen IaaS provider, e.g. on what level of trust they should place within Cloud storage, which forms of Cloud storage are persistent and which are not, etc. If you don't train your developers on the security implications of working in a multi-tenant environment, don't be surprised if they leave your application – and so your organisation – exposed.

Security Operations

The Security Operations service grouping is the last of the major elements of the SRM to be considered. *Figure 25* shows the Security Operations section of the SRM.

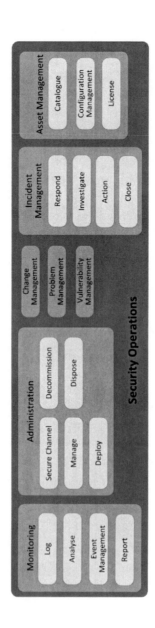

Figure 25: The Security Operations service grouping from the SRM

As can be seen from *Figure 25*, the Security Operations grouping includes a number of different capabilities:

* Monitoring
* Administration
* Incident Management
* Asset Management
* Vulnerability Management
* Change Management
* Problem Management.

Within the IaaS SRM, Monitoring is assigned to be a joint delivery responsibility. Whilst the consumer is responsible for the security monitoring of everything from the operating system upwards, the CSP is responsible for the security monitoring of the underlying physical infrastructure. The Monitoring service grouping includes a number of different services to provide a cohesive approach to security monitoring. The Log service is conceptually responsible for capturing the information required to identify (and then investigate) any security incident, or to meet compliance-driven auditing requirements. Information must be captured at all relevant levels; this includes those areas within the control of the CSP, such as those relating to the physical infrastructure (firewalls, network IPS, storage, etc.) and those areas that are the responsibility of the consumer (the operating system, host-based IPS and firewalls, database, application, etc.) I would recommend that consumers try to ascertain the levels of logging undertaken by their CSPs. The most likely source for this information is the ISO27001 statement of applicability or scoping document for a SAS70 (or ISAE3402/SSAE16) assessment.

Logging is only the beginning of a true security monitoring capability. The logged information must then also be securely stored[77] in a forensically sound manner, where possible (in case it must later be relied upon in court). The Analyse service is responsible for identifying events of interest within the logged information. This is likely to involve the collection, normalisation and correlation of the logs from the different sources mentioned above. This is where an obvious weakness of the Public Cloud model approach becomes apparent. A consumer of a Public Cloud CSP can only collate information from the operating system level upward – they have no visibility of the information logged by their CSP. This weakness is not present with the Private Cloud approach, and may be less of an issue with a Community Cloud. One advantage of the IaaS model – when compared with the PaaS and SaaS models – is that consumers can often use the same security monitoring agents within their Cloud-based virtualised environment as they use within their own data centres. Depending on your willingness to accept security event information coming from outside of your trusted domain, you could also simply reuse existing collation and analysis points within your on-premise security architecture. If your posture is more risk averse, a separate collation point for information sourced from Cloud systems could be implemented, either on-premise or on-Cloud. To reduce costs, it may be prudent to implement a single collation and analysis point (subject to scalability) that is able to monitor events across all of your Cloud-based services. This logging and analysis point should be separated from your secure, trusted domain.

---

[77] The Storage service resides within the Hosting service grouping in the SRM.

Once the information has been collated, it must usually be normalised to a common form to enable more effective correlation and analysis. The Analyse service must then examine the logged and normalised information and highlight any events of interest – be these potential security incidents or other pre-configured events. At this point, the Event Management services should kick in. The purpose of the Event Management service is to recognise the next point of escalation for an event; this could be a case of no action required or escalation to either the Incident Management (for security issues) or Problem Management services. The final service within the Monitoring service is the Report service – which is as simple as it sounds. The Report service is for enabling reports to be produced from the Monitoring service. It should be possible for both the raw log information and the output from the Analyse service to be securely produced and exported from the Monitoring service via the Report service.

There are some IaaS-specific elements in the Monitoring service grouping that consumers should consider:

- Communication channels must be available both to and from the CSP in the event of a security incident requiring one party to notify the other.
- Tools, such as Catbird, HyTrust, etc. can be used to log and monitor the information flows across the hypervisor (this is typically more relevant to Private Cloud approaches).
- Consumers need to investigate the logging options available within the specific Cloud services that they are adopting. Log information may be available beneath the operating system level. For example, AWS S3

enables access log records to be created, which capture details of requests to access stored objects[78].

Security monitoring is a vital part of any security regime. I view it as even more important where the services and data are hosted outside of your secure, trusted, domain.

Administration

The Administration service grouping includes those activities typically associated with system administration roles: deploying new services, managing those services whilst in operation, and then decommissioning and disposing of the relevant kit when the service reaches the end of its life. As the SRM reflects an application security architecture, the majority of these administrative tasks remain the primary delivery responsibility of the consumer in an SRM context. Whilst CSP staff are responsible for the physical deployment and management of the physical hardware, the consumer retains responsibility for the management and deployment from the operating system upwards (including their virtual networking). The Administration service grouping includes the following services:

- **Secure Channel:** The Secure Channel service provides a secure communications path between the relevant system administrator and the server, database or application that they manage. With IaaS services, access to the console will likely be physically implemented via

---

[78] *http://aws.amazon.com/s3/faqs/#Does_Amazon_S3_support_data_access_audit.*

SSH (secure shell). Some providers (e.g. ElasticHosts) will also provide VNC (remote desktop) access to Cloud services, whilst others provide web-based console access (Rackspace). Some providers will also provide the ability to rent dedicated virtual private network connections into their virtualised environments, e.g. the Amazon Direct Connect service. From the operating system upwards, it is the responsibility of the consumer to implement suitable secure communication channels for their administrators; I recommend the use of TLS or SSH encryption as a minimum for such activities.

- **Manage:** The Manage service delivers the capabilities for day-to-day administration activities – e.g. patching, with regard to operating systems, applications, etc. Consumers should consider how they wish to manage their Cloud-based services – do they wish to simply extend their existing processes, or do they wish to adopt some more tailored services for operating with IaaS-based servers? If the latter, then consumers should consider the use of tools, such as Puppet[79], RightScale[80] and CohesiveFT's Elastic Server[®81], which enable the configuration and deployment of virtual machine images across on-premise and multiple IaaS Cloud providers from a single interface.

- **Deploy:** The Deploy service, much like the Manage service, requires a number of underlying logical services to deliver the conceptual functionality of deploying new services onto a Cloud service. Many of

---

[79] *http://puppetlabs.com/puppet/puppet-enterprise/*.
[80] *www.rightscale.com*.
[81] *www.cohesiveft.com/elastic_server/main/elastic_server_home*.

these services would be drawn from other areas of the SRM – including the Risk Management, Test, Configuration Management and Architecture & Design services. In addition to the deployment of virtual machine images, the Deploy service would also be responsible for the deployment of application code onto the Cloud. This entails the usual processes around release management, so as to ensure a smooth migration to a new or updated version of code. Given the ease with which virtual servers can be initiated, great care must be taken to manage the proliferation of unnecessary running images – a problem similar to the well-known issue of image sprawl in virtualised environments. The difference in the Cloud environment is that unnecessary images will all be charged back to the consumer – pay as you go is only advantageous if you are actually using the resources you have active.

- **Decommission:** The Decommission service is the polar opposite of the Deploy service. Once an application or server has reached the end of its usefulness, it should be decommissioned. The ease of releasing resources, such as storage and compute, is one of the strengths of the Cloud (or even just virtualisation) model over physical environments. However, decommissioning is a joint delivery responsibility. Consumers need to ensure that they have implemented formal procedures governing the decommissioning of Cloud-based applications and virtual servers. Given the simplicity of shutting down virtual servers in an IaaS environment, it is easy to mistakenly take down a virtual environment that is still in use – either by accident or through the misunderstanding of other applications making use of the same virtual infrastructure. Decommission is a joint delivery responsibility, as it is only the CSP that can ensure that virtualised resources are released cleanly and that no information will leak from the releasing consumer to the next consumer making use of the same physical resources. Consumers should be comfortable with the statements provided by their CSPs regarding how they prevent information leakage when resources are released or when consumers decide to terminate their relationship with the CSP.

- **Dispose:** The Dispose service is firmly within the domain of the CSP. In a Private Cloud environment, the CSP and consumer may be one and the same. The purpose of the Dispose service is to securely dispose of hardware or media when necessary – e.g. upon failure or reaching end of life. Consumers should be comfortable that their data is not at risk of entering the public domain when, for example, their CSP disposes of, or recycles, their storage devices.

Change Management

The Change Management service (at both the consumer and CSP ends) should follow normal established best practices, as documented within ITIL®[82] and elsewhere. Given the potentially volatile nature of Cloud services – due to the rapid provisioning and subsequent release of resources, for example – consumers adopting Cloud services must have change management processes that are capable of reacting to such change requests efficiently and effectively. The need to manage change does not disappear when moving to the Cloud – change just needs to be managed at a speed that

---

[82] *www.itil-officialsite.com/.*

does not compromise the flexibility and agility that the Cloud model offers.

Problem Management

As with Change Management, Cloud consumers and CSPs should adopt accepted best practices with regard to problem management. It is vital that appropriate communications mechanisms are in place to enable the appropriate allocation of responsibilities in the event of a problem. For example, many CSPs maintain web pages and Twitter feeds dedicated to the status of their services. Examples include:

- *www.gogridstatus.com*
- *http://twitter.com/flexiscalesvc*
- *http://status.elastichosts.com/*
- *http://status.apps.rackspace.com/*
- *http://status.aws.amazon.com/*.

Such information feeds enable consumers to identify when a problem is within their remit to fix or when the problem is wider, affecting the IaaS as a whole. CSPs must also offer adequate support contacts to enable their consumers to raise new problems as and when they occur.

Vulnerability Management

The Vulnerability Management service is responsible for delivering a cohesive and comprehensive approach to managing the vulnerabilities associated with a Cloud-based application. Remediation activities that may result from vulnerability management processes should be passed to the relevant risk management and then onwards to the change management services elsewhere within the SRM. The Vulnerability Management service in the SRM is primarily tasked to identify appropriate vulnerability management approaches and then implement these to actively identify vulnerabilities. At a high level, similar vulnerability management strategies should be adopted, whether an application is being hosted on-premise or on the Cloud. Ideally, applications should be tested prior to entering production, and then again at regular intervals (depending upon the criticality of the application) and after any major changes are made to the application or underlying components, such as databases or operating systems. The problem with this approach, when working with Public Cloud providers, is the need to obtain specific permission to conduct vulnerability assessments – or more intrusive penetration tests – on your application. Testing can thus be delayed, depending on how slick the penetration authorisation process is at your CSP. At the minimum, it adds an extra process step to your deployment activities. As an example of the terms and conditions that are common across the IaaS space, we have an extract from the Rackspace Acceptable Usage Policy (UAP) below:

You may not attempt to probe, scan, penetrate or test the vulnerability of a Rackspace Cloud system or network or to breach the Rackspace Cloud's security or authentication measures, whether by passive or intrusive techniques, without the Rackspace Cloud's express written consent.[83]

---

[83] www.rackspace.com/cloud/legal/aup.

Fortunately, CSPs are, in general, aware of their clients' need to test the security of their applications, and are typically supportive of such tests taking place. Amazon, for example, will allow vulnerability scans of their customers' own instances to be made (although no attempts must be made to access resources outside of the relevant customer's environment), and approval for such scans can be sought in advance through the completion of a form made available on their website[84]. There is also another option, which is to make use of a pre-approved vulnerability assessment service. For example, Core offer their CloudInspect® service on the AWS EC2 Cloud, which is:

> ... pre-authorized by Amazon, so you can conduct security tests at your convenience and as frequently as you require[85]

If organisations are more interested in configuration checks – e.g. checks for missing patches and common misconfigurations, such as the use of default username/password combinations – then such checks could be performed without having to notify the CSP, using some of the tools already mentioned in this book (e.g. Catbird and Sentrigo (for databases)).

Once vulnerabilities have been identified, the Vulnerability Management must then route these vulnerabilities via the Co-ordinate service to those other services in the SRM that are designed to decide on the most appropriate course of action.

---

[84] *https://aws-portal.amazon.com/gp/aws/html-forms-controller/contactus/ AWSSecurityPenTestRequest* – a valid AWS account is required to access this page.
[85] *https://aws.amazon.com/solution-providers/isv/core-security-1330979368*.

Incident Management

Consumer Incident Management services for Cloud-based applications should follow traditional processes. Within the SRM, I have defined four services relating to incident management:

- Respond
- Investigate
- Action
- Close.

The Respond service handles the initial triage aspect of incident response. The Event Management service identifies events of interest, and, if they are suspected of indicating security incidents, passes them to the Incident Management service. The Incident Management service should also take feeds from CSP status updates and wider industry alerts (e.g. those concerning widespread virus or worm activity), and respond appropriately. The Respond service must, therefore, incorporate an appropriate communications mechanism for receiving or obtaining notifications, passing these notifications on to the relevant staff, and initiating the creation of an incident log. The other main responsibility of the Respond service is to establish an appropriate group of incident response personnel drawn from the relevant technical areas (e.g. those working at the operating system, database, and application levels), and appoint an appropriate business stakeholder authorised to make decisions on behalf of the business. Decisions to either close down an affected service or leave it running, pending an investigation, should only be taken in full knowledge of the business impact, and should be at the discretion of the business – and not the technology – function.

The Investigate service forms the main part of the overall Incident Management service. The initial tasks of the Investigate service are to contain the incident, and then gather sufficient evidence to enable an informed investigation to take place. In order to contain an incident, you must have thorough knowledge of the application at hand and the systems with which the application interacts – each of which may also have been compromised. Examine logs for indications of unusual activity, and, where possible, conduct passive (i.e. non-interactive) investigations (e.g. on output from network monitoring tools), so as not to tip off an attacker that their activities have been detected. All aspects of this initial investigation must be recorded in the incident log. Once you have an idea of the likely scope of the compromise, you can make a more informed decision as to how the incident should be contained – whether or not the service should be taken down, whether certain communication lines should be cut to prevent further contamination, or whether everything should be left as it is to enable further monitoring of the activities of the attacker, for example. Once you have decided on your containment approach, it is time to begin a more thorough investigation.

Where possible, evidence should be obtained in a forensically sound manner; this may not, however, be possible in an IaaS environment without extensive co-operation from your CSP. Whilst working in an IaaS environment may make obtaining forensically sound evidence more problematic, there is a definite advantage in being able to snapshot, and then analyse, a virtual machine image on a machine that is suspected of being compromised. As ever, with incident response, you need to be aware of the consequences of your activities; keep an eye out for a change in the behaviour of the attacker that may indicate a realisation that they have been detected. A deeply embedded attacker may be quite destructive in their attempts to cover their tracks if they believe they have been spotted, which could lead to a longer down time and a more drawn-out investigation. Ensure that you capture all of your activities in the incident log – such logs are vital evidence, should you wish to pursue criminal charges against the attacker. The purpose of the Analyse service is to identify exactly which information assets have been affected and which attack vector(s) were used to infiltrate the service, and then to identify how to remediate the exploited vulnerabilities, so that a cleanup can begin without the fear that the service will immediately be re-hacked when it is brought back online. This is where the benefit of the virtual image snapshot really comes into its own. The snapshot should contain volatile aspects – e.g. process address spaces in memory that can be difficult to obtain in a physical server without destroying the evidence. Once you are content that you have obtained all of the information you need about the compromise, it is time to pass the relevant information across to the Action service.

The Action service is responsible for implementing the activities needed to recover from an incident. This will involve working with other services within the SRM – e.g. problem and change management, vulnerability management, and others – to make the necessary changes in a managed manner. Likely activities will include the restoration of data from back-ups known to be reliable (i.e. dating from before the compromise), the application of security patches to operating systems or vulnerable applications, and some penetration testing to ensure that the system is no longer vulnerable to the identified attack vector(s). In an IaaS scenario, it is advisable to rebuild machine images from scratch, rather than attempting to fix compromised images; this enables you to build from a trusted starting point.

The Close service is responsible for ensuring that the incident log has been completed satisfactorily and for storing the log in a secure manner. Furthermore, the Close service must also capture any lessons learned during the incident response process; this helps to avoid making the same mistakes twice, but also helps to spread good practice where certain activities have been shown to work well.

Asset Management

The Asset Management service grouping reflects the need for a consumer to account for their information assets, even where those assets reside in an IaaS Cloud.

The first aspect of the Asset Management service grouping is the Catalogue service. The purpose of the Catalogue service is to establish an asset register containing information assets relevant to the application. This register should include references to the relevant virtual machine images, storage locations and software images, etc. The next aspect of the Asset Management grouping is the License service; many software vendors offer specific licensing terms for implementation in Cloud services. Consumers must ensure that they have the correct licenses for operating their software in a virtualised Cloud environment. Consumers should carefully investigate the terms and conditions for any software that they plan to implement in order to determine whether or not the license terms are appropriate for a Cloud implementation. They should, for example, ask: how do the terms and conditions account for the elasticity inherent in the Cloud? Do the vendors charge for maximum peak usage, or on a pay-as you-go basis? Do the vendors charge per virtual machine or virtual core? Do the vendors even support implementation in a Cloud environment?

The final aspect of the Asset Management service grouping is Configuration Management. Configuration Management is as important in an IaaS (or other virtualised) environment as it is where dealing with physical hardware. One issue that must not be forgotten when dealing with IaaS Clouds is that of the patching of currently redundant images. Given the elastic nature of Cloud services, it may be that machine images are deactivated and then stored for future use after a spike in usage. Alternatively, those using Cloud services for development and testing may not require their images to be constantly active. The issue here is that these currently inactive images could, if containing unpatched vulnerabilities, present a security risk to your virtualised infrastructure when they are activated. Configuration management is not just about patching, however. It is important to know the overall state and usage of your IaaS services – not only from a security perspective, but also from a billing reconciliation perspective. Cloud is normally charged on a pay-per-use basis; consumers should check, every so often, that these charges are accurate.

Conclusion

This chapter has provided some practical advice regarding the implementation of the security services described within the SRM for an IaaS environment. In addition to the guidance provided in this book, consumers should also consider the guidance provided by the CSPs themselves. Most CSPs now offer whitepapers, or devote sections on their websites to describing their security capabilities. Examples include:

- *http://aws.amazon.com/security/*
- *http://go.gogrid.com/whitepapers/gogrid-cloud-security*
- *http://broadcast.rackspace.com/downloads/pdfs/Rackspa ceSecurityApproach.pdf.*

I recommend that those considering the use of a CSP closely examine the information that the CSP provides on their security processes, and take advantage of any offers to provide further detail, typically under NDAs.

CHAPTER 10: SECURITY AND PLATFORM AS A SERVICE

This chapter describes how the security services defined within the security reference model (SRM) shown in *Figure 7* may be delivered by consumers implementing an application upon a Platform as a Service Cloud.

Whilst I may occasionally provide examples of the security services offered by PaaS providers, it is not my intention to provide a comprehensive overview of any particular PaaS platform. Similarly, I am not attempting to provide an exhaustive catalogue of available PaaS solutions. As with the rest of this book, my aim is to help you to adopt a way of working that enables you to find the most appropriate solution for your own particular set of requirements, rather than to specify how security must be delivered. As we move up the stack from IaaS, through PaaS towards SaaS, the diversity of the Cloud solutions increases – and so security solutions must become increasingly tailored to the situation at hand.

The OpenCrowd taxonomy[86] of Cloud services splits PaaS CSPs into a number of different categories:

- Business intelligence – examples including:
  - K2 Analytics (*http://k2analytics.com/*)
  - GoodData (*www.gooddata.com*).

- Database – examples including:

---

[86] *http://cloudtaxonomy.opencrowd.com/taxonomy/platform-as-a-service/*.

- o Kognitio (*www.kognitio.com*)
- o Amazon Relational Database Service (*http://aws.amazon.com/rds/*)
- o Amazon SimpleDB (*http://aws.amazon.com/simpledb/*)
- o Cloudant (*www.cloudant.com*)
- o Database.com (*www.database.com/*).

- • Development and testing – examples including:
  - o CollabNet (*www.open.collab.net*)
  - o Keynote Systems (*www.keynote.com*).

- • Integration – examples including:
  - o Apigee (*www.apigee.com*)
  - o Boomi (*www.boomi.com*)
  - o IBM Cast Iron (*www-01.ibm.com/software/integration/cast-iron-cloud-integration/#*)
  - o Cordys (*www.cordys.com*)
  - o Eloqua (*http://appcloud.eloqua.com/*).

- • General purpose – examples including:
  - o Force.com (*www.force.com*)
  - o Google App Engine (*http://code.google.com/appengine/*)
  - o Azure (*www.windowsazure.com/en-us*)
  - o Heroku (*www.heroku.com*)
  - o Cloud Foundry (*www.cloudfoundry.com*).

I will focus upon the latter category in this book – those CSPs that provide one or more run-times within which consumers can deploy applications.

PaaS and the SRM

The rest of this chapter is dedicated to explaining how the services described within the SRM can be delivered when deploying services on a PaaS Cloud. As discussed in *Chapter 7*, PaaS can be the most complex of the Cloud service models to secure, due to the amount of cross-over between CSPs and consumers in the provision of security services. Consumers must make sure that they are aware of, and address, potential gaps between the aspects of security services delivered by the CSP and the aspects delivered by the consumer themselves.

Secure Development

With the PaaS service model, the Secure Development services are very much a joint delivery responsibility. Whilst Cloud consumers are directly responsible for the security of the code that they develop to run within a PaaS run-time, the CSPs are directly responsible for the security of the code underpinning the run-time, together with the code delivering any PaaS-specific APIs. What does this mean in practice? No matter how secure the code is that a consumer develops, the application could still be vulnerable to application-level exploits targeting problems with the code of the PaaS provider. However, this is a risk that many organisations currently face in more traditional deployments; most major systems will include a few proprietary closed-source applications within their technology stack. Any issues with these applications could also place the overall system at risk. So, whilst the use of code provided by PaaS services may represent a risk, this is only an extension of the risks that organisations are used to managing rather than something completely new.

In terms of general good practice regarding the implementation of a secure development life cycle, I recommend taking a look at the variety of SDL documentation made available by Microsoft at *www.microsoft.com/sdl*.

The SDL processes adopted by Microsoft have helped to rehabilitate the company's reputation from a security perspective. Many years ago, the security of Microsoft products was often the butt of jokes amongst the security research community; this is no longer the case. The efforts that Microsoft has made to develop its software more securely – and also respond to vulnerabilities more co-operatively, when they are discovered – have led to Microsoft now being viewed as something of an exemplar amongst its peers.

Coding Standards

Since such platforms as Azure, Heroku and the Google App Engine support standard languages, such as Java, Ruby, Python® and C#, you should be able to use many of the standard secure development processes associated with the relevant languages. Life may be more difficult for those adopting PaaS services using proprietary languages, such as the Apex® language[87] offered by Force.com, as a whole new set of coding standards will need to be created. In either situation, you should standardise which PaaS-provided APIs you adopt (e.g. access control and cryptographic APIs), and where you code – or otherwise implement – your own equivalent functionality.

---

[87] *http://wiki.developerforce.com/page/Apex*.

For the sake of clarity, I shall highlight that Force.com is the PaaS offering of Salesforce.com. In fact, Force.com is the platform that supports the Salesforce.com SaaS application itself, and so consumers have access to services of proven scale and utility. Salesforce.com has made significant quantities of documentation available for developers via their wiki. The main section devoted to security can be found at *http://wiki.developerforce.com/page/Security*.

The Force.com wiki includes some specific secure coding guidelines at *http://wiki.developerforce.com/page/Secure_Coding_Guideline*.

These secure coding guidelines offer developers advice and guidance on how to avoid common security weaknesses and how to implement common security controls, including[88]:

1. Cross-site scripting
2. S(O)QL injection
3. Cross-site request forgery
4. Secure communications and cookies
5. Storing secrets
6. Arbitrary redirects
7. Access control
8. Enforcing CRUD and FLS (Force.com)
9. SSO for composite apps.

In addition to the documented guidance, more practical assistance is also available via the OWASP Enterprise Security API (ESAPI). ESAPI is a free, open source library

---

[88] Taken from *http://wiki.developerforce.com/page/Secure_Coding_Guideline*.

that incorporates functions to handle input validation, output encoding and access control for Force.com objects (using CRUD/FLS and Sharing[89]). The ESAPI library is available from *http://code.google.com/p/force-dot-com-esapi/*.

The Windows® Azure platform boasts a number of platform-specific security features – the AppFabric Access Control Service, for example, which provides federated authentication and authorisation services for REST[90] web services. Microsoft have produced a document entitled, *Security Best Practices For Developing Windows Azure Applications*, 2010, which describes the security services offered by the Azure platform and provides guidance on the development of secure applications on the Azure PaaS. This document is available from *http://go.microsoft.com/?linkid=9751405&clcid=0x409*.

Users making use of PaaS providers, such as Heroku or the Google App Engine, should adopt typical best practices for the languages that they are using, but must also bear in mind any peculiarities of their chosen delivery platform in terms of data storage, concurrency, etc.

The other two services forming the Secure Development service grouping of the SRM are Code Review and Unit Test. In general, the requirements for these two services are independent of the chosen delivery model – code should be reviewed against the implemented coding standards and subject to unit tests to ensure that it delivers against the specified requirements, including those of a security nature.

---

[89] CRUD/FLS and Sharing will be discussed in the Access Management section of this Chapter.
[90] *www.ics.uci.edu/~fielding/pubs/dissertation/rest_arch_style.htm*.

Integrity

As with the vast majority of service groupings within the SRM, the Integrity service grouping is a joint delivery responsibility split between the CSP and the consumer. The CSP must ensure that it has sufficient controls in place to provide sufficient levels of non-repudiation, with regard to activities affecting the platform. For example, CSPs should maintain strict audit and process controls when making changes to the systems underlying their platform. Similarly, CSPs should ensure that sufficient content checking is in place to prevent their systems (including management systems) becoming infected with malware.

Consumers of PaaS services must also build in their own Non-Repudiation services where required by their application. As we are currently considering applications hosted on PaaS Clouds, the consumer still has the opportunity to code whichever non-repudiation controls are required. This may range from simple logging and auditing of user activities through to the use of digital signatures provided via cryptographic services.

Content checking is more complicated within a PaaS environment than within an IaaS environment. Whereas standard anti-virus packages may be implemented within virtualised servers on an IaaS Cloud (subject to licensing), this is not the case with a PaaS. However, this does not mean that consumers are unable to implement content checking for their PaaS-hosted applications. There are two main options: firstly, the PaaS-hosted application could redirect all content for import (and perhaps export, depending on business requirements) to an on-premise or IaaS-hosted standard content-checking application. The second approach would be to make use of a SaaS anti-virus provider, such as Scanii[91] or Virustotal[92]. In this second scenario, the files to be checked are provided to the anti-virus SaaS, and an answer is returned indicating whether the file is clean or infected. Obviously, this does not emulate a fully featured anti-virus solution (e.g. there is no eradication capability), but it does, however, enable consumers to detect malicious content before it is acted upon or stored within "trusted" data stores. The Scanii service adopts a REST-based approach and enables consumers to direct Scanii to pull content from REST-based Storage services, such as AWS S3, rather than requiring the relevant content to always be pushed for checking. This requires a certain amount of trust to be placed in the SaaS provider, as the consumer would be giving them access to their storage account for content-checking purposes.

The Snapshot service is interesting in the PaaS environment, given the potential distributions of data and application code. For example, your data may be stored using the platform's own storage mechanisms, kept on-premise, or, perhaps, hosted using a different Storage as a Service provider (e.g. Amazon S3). Similarly, your application code may be stored on the platform or elsewhere. The executable code itself must exist on the PaaS in order for your application to run.

Consumers must, therefore, consider where each element of their service is located, and then derive appropriate mechanisms to obtain snapshots, where required. As an example, the Windows® Azure Blob storage facility offers

---

[91] *https://scanii.com/.*
[92] *https://www.virustotal.com/faq/.*

the capability to take a read-only snapshot of a "blob"[93]. This capability can be valuable, as Azure Drive[94] virtual hard drives are implemented using blobs; you can, therefore, use blob snapshots to take a snapshot of the state of the virtual hard drives.

With respect to application source code, I recommend that consumers continue to use their existing source code repositories to store audited snapshots of their codebase. Where such code is compiled on-premise and then launched in the Cloud, I would also recommend storing a copy of the compiled executable. This can be more troublesome in platforms like the Heroku platform, where executables ("slugs" in the Heroku context[95]) are compiled within the PaaS. This is potentially troublesome, as it means that consumers lose traceability of the integrity of their code at an earlier stage of deployment then they would in an on-premise or IaaS deployment, where consumers can trace an executable directly back to the source.

Availability

The Availability grouping of the SRM consists of services relating to Business Continuity (BC), Disaster Recovery (DR), Back-up and Failover.

There are fewer options for providing (relatively) seamless business continuity and disaster recovery capabilities with PaaS than there are for IaaS. Whereas it is feasible to switch compute workloads across IaaS providers in the

---

[93] *http://msdn.microsoft.com/en-us/library/hh488361.aspx.*
[94] *www.windowsazure.com/en-us/develop/net/fundamentals/cloud-storage/#drives.*
[95] *http://devcenter.heroku.com/articles/slug-compiler.*

event of an incident (as described in *Chapter 9*), it is not feasible to perform a similar failover between PaaS providers. Consider the Force.com platform, for example, where consumers implement applications in the proprietary Apex language. Other Cloud providers may have an abundance of compute and storage resources, but not the ability to execute applications written in Apex. Consumers cannot, therefore, simply "lift and shift" their application and data from the Force.com platform to a competing PaaS in the event of a major outage at Force.com. Force.com consumers (and most other PaaS consumers) are, therefore, reliant upon the resilience of the services offered by their providers.

In the interests of fairness, I should note that Force.com maintains high levels of availability (above 99.9%). It is those consumers who are concerned about the remaining 0.1% of unplanned downtime, or those using less reliable PaaS providers, that need to manage the residual risk. One approach may be to maintain a copy of the underlying business data within another CSP alongside a cut-down application providing the bare-bones business capabilities sufficient to keep your business operational whilst either your main CSP recovers, or you find, a more permanent solution. This approach would, obviously, incur costs with respect to the development of such a bare-bones application, and a possible transformation of data into non-proprietary formats. There would also be recurring costs with regard to ongoing storage requirements. Enterprises need to consider these costs in the context of the unavailability of their application over a variety of timeframes. For example, such an approach may be overkill if a service was only unavailable for a matter of minutes. But would this still be overkill if the PaaS-hosted application was to be unavailable for a matter of hours, days, or perhaps even longer? Consider both the potential business impact and the likelihood of the event occurring, and use this analysis to drive your approach towards business continuity and disaster recovery.

Now, although PaaS providers do not tend to offer 99.999% uptime service levels, they do tend to provide their consumers with managed run-times that aim to maintain availability of the applications that they host. For example, the Heroku model involves running processes ("dynos") within their run-time, known as the "dyno manifold". The dyno manifold restarts crashed processes without intervention from the consumer, and can move dynos to new locations automatically, should there be a failure in the underlying hardware[96]. Such capabilities can be expensive to implement in an on-premise environment.

Of course, one of the perceived advantages of the Cloud model is the ability to dynamically scale resources to meet spikes in processing requirements. This ability enables organisations to maintain the availability of their applications in the face of increased demand or, potentially, to cope with denial-of-service attacks. Heroku enables its consumers to scale their application up (and down) via the "scale" command, as documented at *http://devcenter.heroku.com/articles/scaling*.

Scaling is automatic within the Google App Engine, subject to quota limits, as explained at *http://code.google.com/appengine/docs/quotas.html*.

---

[96] *http://devcenter.heroku.com/articles/erosion-resistance*.

Whilst the Google App Engine approach is desirable from an overhead perspective, it can cause problems if you breach your quota. At this point, the service becomes unavailable. Fortunately, the Google quotas are generous and, if you do find that the default quotas are not sufficient, they can be increased in negotiation with Google. The Google App Engine also includes an anti-denial-of-service (anti-DoS) capability, which enables consumers to blacklist IP addresses and subnets; the application then drops requests for these before they are processed. This capability is explained further at *http://code.google.com/appengine/docs/java/config/dos.html*.

It should be noted that the Cloud model does introduce a new form of denial-of-service vulnerability. Whereas traditional DDoS attacks tend to rely on the exhaustion of resources – such as network or compute resources – DDoS on the Cloud can focus on economic exhaustion. Cloud is pay as you go, so, by forcing their victims to use more Cloud-based resources, attackers can rapidly increase the costs associated with those resources. Where there are set budget limits, a denial of service can result, once the budget has been exceeded. This type of attack is known as an economic denial of service.

Consumers can automatically scale the resources that they consume on the Azure platform through the use of the Autoscaling Application Block[97]. The Autoscaling Application Block allows consumers to configure a set of rules and constraints governing the resources allocated to their applications. As an example, Azure consumers can allocate additional resources, during set periods of time, in

---

[97] *http://msdn.microsoft.com/en-us/library/hh680881(v=pandp.50).aspx.*

order to cope with regular peaks in activity (e.g. at first thing in the morning). This type of configurable functionality enables consumers to deliver the elasticity and cost-savings that Cloud has always promised.

Another advantage over on-premise deployments that PaaS services tend to share with IaaS services is the ease of data replication across multiple data centres. For example, an interesting default feature of Azure is the way that customer data stored in blobs, tables or queues is automatically replicated to six different storage areas (three in one data centre and three more in another data centre within the same region) to provide resilience. Such features are designed from a resilience perspective, rather than a data back-up perspective. PaaS consumers must continue to maintain separate (off-platform) data back-ups, where required. Another important data-related aspect of Cloud provision is ensuring that you understand the persistence of the data storage solution you are adopting. As an example, I've already introduced the blob and table storage options within Azure, but Azure also offers "local storage" and the blob-backed virtual hard drives known as "Azure drives"[98]. For the "local storage" option, virtual hard drives associated with the virtual machine hosting the application are used. Data stored using "local storage" can be configured to either persist through a VM reboot, or to be erased whenever the VM reboots. However, should the Azure management systems move an application from one VM to another VM (e.g. to manage a hardware failure), Azure will not transfer the data stored on the local storage of the original VM to the new VM. The original data will be

---

[98] *www.windowsazure.com/en- us/develop/net/fundamentals/cloud-storage/.*

effectively lost to the application. Consumers should, therefore, not use "local storage" for data that requires long-term storage. From an availability and back-up perspective, you must ensure that you understand the underlying data storage mechanisms, and choose the ones most appropriate to your requirements.

There is one final point I will make in consideration of Availability and the PaaS approach. Although PaaS consumers are, typically, unaware of the underlying virtual machines[99], the availability of the platform is intrinsically dependent upon the availability of such virtual machines and the underlying infrastructure. As an example, the Heroku PaaS is built upon the Amazon Web Services EC2 IaaS. The availability of the Heroku PaaS is, therefore, dependent upon the availability of the underlying Amazon Web Services. This is a good example of where consumers need to be aware of the overall supply chain. Consumers should extend their due diligence activities to any underlying Cloud services in addition to their investigation of the front-end Cloud service.

Cryptography

As with the other Cloud service models, if you find that the Cloud service provider staff pose a threat to the confidentiality of your data, you must consider encrypting your data before it enters the Cloud. Encrypting data after it enters the Cloud leaves a window of opportunity, whereby your data is in the Cloud, in the clear, prior to encryption.

---

[99] Azure is a notable exception; consumers can use Azure VM roles to deploy custom Windows® Server 2008 R2 images.

Furthermore, encrypting data in the Cloud means that your encryption key is also in the Cloud. If you're using symmetric encryption (where the encryption and decryption keys are one and the same), this means that a compromise of the Cloud service may provide access to both your encrypted data and the decryption key. However, the issue with encrypting your data on-premise is that it leaves your data in a state where it is difficult to work with from an application perspective – unless the application has access to the appropriate decryption key. This approach removes the security advantage of encrypting on-premise.

Consumers should, therefore, consider how their data is to be used by their application (or end-users), and then secure the data appropriately – either by encryption on-premise or by encryption on-Cloud (where necessary).

Now, the selling point of the PaaS service model is that it abstracts away the infrastructure issues, whilst still providing consumers with the flexibility to build and deploy applications of their own choosing or design. In an IaaS environment, consumers have complete freedom to incorporate whichever standard encryption libraries[100] they like into their Cloud-based application. In a PaaS environment, the choice of cryptographic libraries available to the on-PaaS application is limited to the cryptographic libraries provided by the PaaS or to the languages supported by the PaaS. Fortunately, many PaaS providers have recognised the importance of encryption, and provide access to cryptographic functionality.

---

[100] It is generally a security anti-pattern to implement your own cryptographic libraries.

The Force.com platform has the Apex Crypto class, which provides applications with the capability to encrypt and decrypt information, generate hash values, create digital signatures and generate signed hash values (message authentication codes). The Crypto class supports a number of different hashing algorithms, including MD5[101], SHA-1, SHA-256 and SHA-512. AES-128, AES-192 and AES-256 are available for data encryption. More information on the Force.com Apex Crypto class can be found at *http://wiki.developerforce.com/page/Apex_Crypto_Class*.

Consumers of Windows® Azure have access to the Cryptographic service providers built into the Microsoft® .NET® framework. Similarly, consumers of other PaaS services can make use of the crypto libraries that they are using.

When using cryptographic libraries in the Cloud, it is crucial that the keys are secured appropriately – usually through the use of secure storage capabilities, e.g. Protected Custom Settings[102] in the Force.com platform. Consumers should ensure that they meet the requirements dictated for the conceptual Key Management service in the SRM.

So far, I have only introduced the data encryption aspects of cryptography. The other common encryption aspect related to Cloud-hosted applications is the encryption of data in transit, typically through the use of SSL or TLS. Given that one of the common use cases for PaaS is the hosting of customer-facing web applications, PaaS providers have made it fairly straightforward to implement SSL/TLS

---

[101] I would recommend avoiding MD5, where possible.
[102] *http://wiki.developerforce.com/page/Secure_Coding_Storing_Secrets#Apex_and_Visualforce_Applications*.

support within an application. The links below refer to relevant guidance on the implementation of SSL for a number of PaaS providers:

- *www.windowsazure.com/en-us/develop/net/common-tasks/enable-ssl/*
- *http://wiki.developerforce.com/page/Making_Authenticated_Web_Service_Callouts_Using_Two-Way_SSL*[103]
- *http://devcenter.heroku.com/articles/ssl*
- *http://code.google.com/appengine/kb/general.html#https*.

As ever, with SSL or TLS (or other network encryption in general), be aware of the impact of encryption on the capability of your (and your CSP's) network security tools – such as firewalls and intrusion prevention systems. If the traffic is encrypted, it cannot be inspected. Consumers should consider where in their architectures they break SSL connections to ensure that the traffic entering their domain can be inspected prior to processing. For example, SSL traffic could terminate in a specific front-end application, which then forwards the traffic to the main application that would allow inspection of the plain text traffic (via the Content Check service) prior to processing.

Access Management

An extract from the SRM, showing the Access Management service grouping and indicating the primary

---

[103] This refers to securing web service communications between Force.com applications and other services. Page views of Force.com applications by end-users are encrypted via https by default.

delivery responsibility for each service is shown in *Figure 26.*

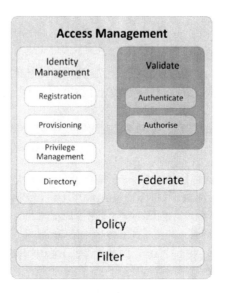

Figure 26: The Access Management services of the SRM.

Yellow implies joint delivery responsibility. Red implies primary delivery responsibility sits with the CSP.

As in *Figure 9*, the red services represent services that are primarily the responsibility of the service provider to deliver, whilst the yellow services represent those that are jointly delivered. *Figure 26* indicates that the majority of the Access Control services are jointly delivered. The Validate services are noted as being the primary delivery responsibility of the CSP. This is based on the assumption that the consumer is making use of authentication and authorisation services provided by the platform. The primary delivery responsibility would shift towards the consumer, should this not be the case.

I will not repeat content that I previously presented in *Chapter 9* – the overviews of OAuth or OpenID, for example. However, both OAuth and OpenID can be relevant to applications hosted on PaaS services.

Before I expand upon the individual Access Management services, I will provide references to CSP documents that describe the access control capabilities of their platforms.

The Windows® Azure platform includes a set of Access Control Services (known as ACSs), which are described at:

- *http://msdn.microsoft.com/library/gg429786.aspx* and
- *www.windowsazure.com/en-us/develop/net/how-to-guides/access-control/*.

ACS offers a number of capabilities that can be mapped onto SRM services. ACS offers the following functionality:

- Federation
- Authentication
- Authorisation
- Security Token Flow and Transformation
- Trust Management
- Administration
- Automation.

The identity management and access control capabilities of the Force.com platform are described at:

- *http://wiki.developerforce.com/page/An_Overview_of_F orce.com_User_Management_and_Sign-on* and
- *http://wiki.developerforce.com/page/Enforcing_CRUD_ and_FLS*.

The first link above describes the Force.com capabilities for user authentication – from username and password through to federated authentication via SAML tokens. The second link explains the data-centric access controls – i.e. the mechanisms available to control user access to data within the Force.com platform.

For those platforms that support Java – e.g. Google App Engine and Heroku – consumers should consider the use of Spring Security to provide their authentication and authorisation services. The following links provide more information on Spring Security:

- *http://static.springsource.org/spring-security/site/* and
- *http://static.springsource.org/spring-security/site/ docs/3.1.x/reference/technical-overview.html*.

It can be more problematic to implement Spring Security for PaaS services than for on-premise applications. For example, Heroku does not currently support session affinity (also known as "sticky sessions"), and uses round robin distribution of user sessions to running dynos[104]. This can lead to the situation where a user that has authenticated to one dyno is redirected to another dyno that runs a separate instance of the same process, but for which the user is no longer authenticated (as the authentication information is

---

[104] *http://devcenter.heroku.com/articles/intro-for-java-developers*.

held with the session state of the original dyno). This second dyno would then, again, need to prompt the user to authenticate. Such issues can usually be worked around – e.g. through the use of a separate state table, as described at *http://grails-plugins.github.com/grails-heroku/docs/ manual/guide/2%20Usage.htmlg.*

So, whilst there may be teething troubles while adopting the use of established frameworks in a PaaS environment, these troubles are likely to be an acceptable price to pay for the benefits of using tried and tested security functions.

Identity Management

The Identity Management services of the SRM include

* Registration
* Provisioning
* Privilege Management
* Directory.

As described in *Chapter 9*, user Registration processes should be independent of the IT delivery mechanisms; the proof of identity required to access your systems is related to the value of your data and the impact of compromise.

The Provisioning mechanisms available to your application vary, depending on the PaaS provider that you choose. For example, with Force.com, users can be directly provisioned via the online Administration Console. Alternatively, Force.com users can programmatically provision new users via the Force.com Web Services API, as explained at *http://wiki.developerforce.com/page/An_Overview_of_Forc e.com_User_Management_and_Sign-on.*

Users of Windows® Azure will, typically, provision their application users via traditional Microsoft technologies, such as Active Directory (which could be hosted on-premise). Users can then be provided with access to the Azure-hosted application via claims-based security, using the Azure Access Control Service and supporting capabilities.

The Privilege Management and Directory aspects of PaaS solutions depend upon the platform chosen and the aspects of that platform that you choose to incorporate within your application.

In terms of Privilege Management and access to the PaaS management capabilities, there are, again, differences in the levels of control available (e.g. the availability of role-based access controls). The Google App Engine, for example, supports three levels of access to the Management Console: "viewer", "developer" and "owner". These are described at *http://code.google.com/appengine/docs/ adminconsole/roles.html*.

The viewer role has read-only access, whereas the owner role has full control of the account.

Force.com offers a privilege model based on the use of profiles and sharing rules. Profiles control what users can see and do within the Force.com platform. Sharing rules enable Force.com administrators to restrict or enlarge the data records available to a user. The Force.com platform controls access to data using a combination of privilege and data-centric mechanisms. Users can be granted Create, Read, Update or Delete permissions to standard (or custom) objects. These CRUD permissions are applied at the profile level to control what activities users can undertake. Organisations requiring more granular control can make use of Field Level Security (FLS) that enables similar CRUD permissions to be enforced on the individual fields within an object. CRUD and FLS controls are explained in more detail at *http://wiki.developerforce.com/page/Enforcing_ CRUD_and_FLS*.

In terms of the provisioning of administrator users, most PaaS platforms will allow you to sign up to access their services with a simple e-mail address (Heroku, for example) or by using an existing account with a separate service (e.g. you could use a Google account to access the Google App Engine). This does raise an important consideration from an enterprise perspective: you should not allow your enterprise PaaS administrators to sign up to Cloud services using their own personal e-mail addresses. If you do, you could find yourself in an uncomfortable position, should one of your administrators choose to find alternative employment – i.e. you could become locked out of your PaaS-hosted applications. You should, instead, create specific e-mail addresses, owned by the enterprise, to be used to register for PaaS services.

Validate

The Validate services of the SRM provide the ability to authenticate and then authorise user access (including that for service users) to your Cloud-based application. In the PaaS model, the CSPs bear primary responsibility for the delivery of the Validate services where the application relies upon the authentication and authorisation services provided by the CSP.

Authenticate

As with applications hosted within IaaS Clouds (discussed in *Chapter 9*), organisations have a number of options for delivering the Authenticate service. PaaS consumers develop their own applications, and so can choose how they authenticate their users. Methods range from the simple use of usernames and passwords through to more complicated mechanisms, such as certificate-based authentication or federated authentication.

The Force.com platform supports username/password authentication by default, but can also support delegated and federated authentication. When using delegated authentication, users enter their credentials on the Force.com log-in page, but the platform then transmits those credentials to an end point configured by the consumer, which then validates the presented credentials. Whilst this approach enables consumers to retain control of their users' credentials (i.e. they are not stored within the Force.com platform), it still requires user credentials to be transmitted across the Internet. Another issue with the delegated authentication approach is the requirement for the consumer to develop an appropriate end point (with access to an identity store and the Internet) to perform the username/password validation. Federated authentication via SAML is a more flexible approach, particularly where a consumer has a requirement to use multi-factor authentication. In this latter scenario, a consumer can make use of an authentication and identity provider, such as CRYPTOCard, to provide multi-factor authentication to their Force.com application.

Access to the Windows® Azure platform can be secured using a variety of different authentication mechanisms:

Active Directory Federation Services (ADFS), the Windows® Identity Foundation, the Access Control Service (ACS) and the .NET framework. RSA recently announced that their SecurID product can now be integrated with ADFS 2.0,[105] which means that access to the Azure platform can now be secured using two-factor authentication. For those applications with more basic security requirements, consumers could consider using ASP .NET forms-based authentication. In this scenario, consumers would typically use Azure Tables storage to provide the identity store. Another option for applications with more basic security requirements is to implement federated authentication, whereby your Azure application uses identity providers, such as Google, Windows® Live or Facebook. This approach would allow your users to access your services by logging in with their Google account or Windows® Live ID, for example. The ACS *How To* guides, providing detailed guidance on how to work with these identity providers, can be found at *http://msdn.microsoft.com/en-us/library/windowsazure/ gg185939.aspx*.

In terms of the authentication of management access to the Azure platform, Microsoft supports the use of x.509 v3 certificates in the form of Management Certificates[106]. These certificates are used to control access to management functionality, including the ability to upload virtual machine images to VM Roles, to use the Azure Service Management REST API, and to use Windows® Azure Tools for Visual Studio to create and manage application deployments.

---

[105] *www.rsa.com/press_release.aspx?id=11567*.
[106] *http://msdn.microsoft.com/en-us/library/windowsazure/gg981935.aspx*.

The Google App Engine platform supports three mechanisms for user authentication: Google Accounts, accounts on your own Google Apps domain, or federated authentication via OpenID (as explained in *Chapter 9*). The first option requires your user to hold a Google account, the second option is limited to those organisations that have implemented Google Apps (*see Chapter 11*), whilst the third option is limited to those consumers who wish to implement federated authentication. Individuals can obtain a Google account simply by signing up with a valid e-mail address. The App Engine authentication options are explored in more detail at *http://code.google.com/appengine/articles/auth.html*.

Google App Engine customers looking to implement multi-factor authentication must do so through the use of an OpenID provider supporting multi-factor authentication.

Authorise

The Authorise service grouping controls what an authenticated user may do within the application – e.g. what data and functions they may access. The authorisation process described within *Figure 18* for IaaS-based applications is equally applicable to PaaS-based applications.

Applications coded to run on the Heroku, Google App Engine or similar platforms will need to incorporate their own authorisation processes – e.g. using Spring Security. Consumers of Azure or Force.com can take advantage of their inbuilt authorisation mechanisms. Within the Force.com platform, authorisation occurs automatically, based upon the CRUD and FLS privileges that they have been assigned – e.g. VisualForce pages will not display objects that users are not authorised to see when accessing via the usual user interface. CRUD and FLS must be enforced manually when using Apex Web Services (as such services are not presented via the VisualForce-delivered user interface)[107].

Windows® Azure offers the aforementioned Access Control Service (ACS) to enforce authorised access to REST-based services. Azure consumers also have access to the usual authorisation controls within the .NET Framework (e.g. IsInRole checks[108]). ACS supports federated authorisation, which will be discussed more thoroughly in the next section.

Federate

Rather than repeat generic federation content from *Chapter 9*, I shall limit the following discussion on federation technologies to those relevant to PaaS services.

The Windows® Azure platform has extensive support for federated authentication and authorisation via claims-based security. Claims-based security refers to the granting of access to an application based upon a specific claim presented by a user request. For example, a simple request could contain a claim that the user originates from a specific geographic region, and so is authorised to access content specific to that region. In order to function, such claims must be issued by a trusted entity and then validated

---

[107] *http://wiki.developerforce.com/page/Enforcing_CRUD_and_FLS.*
[108] *http://msdn.microsoft.com/en-us/library/system.web.security.roleprincipal. isinrole.aspx.*

by the receiving application. The process would typically proceed as follows:

1. A user wishes to access an application.
2. The user contacts a security token service (STS) that is able to create a token containing a relevant claim (e.g. a geographic location claim).
3. The STS verifies that the user meets the criteria to validate their claim. This may just be a case of the STS trusting information provided by an identity provider.
4. If the claim is valid, the STS issues a security token containing the validated claim.
5. The user passes their security token to the desired application, alongside their request for access.
6. The application extracts any relevant claims from the security token.
7. The application passes the claims across to a Policy Decision Point (PDP) to decide whether the claim is sufficient to authorise access.
8. The application grants or denies access based upon the response from the PDP.

Claims-based access control is, therefore, similar to the authorisation process illustrated in *Figure 18* – e.g. in the abstraction of policy decisions from the application. ACS can be used as a security token service to create the tokens based upon information provided by identity providers and rules stored within the ACS rules engine. Claims-based authorisation processes are described in more detail at *http://msdn.microsoft.com/en-us/library/windowsazure/ gg185915.aspx*.

Alternative approaches to claims-based authorisation of Azure applications are outlined at *http://msdn.microsoft.com/en-us/library/windowsazure/ gg185904.aspx*.

Azure supports a number of different identity providers "out of the box", including:

- Windows® Live ID
- Facebook
- Google
- Yahoo
- WS-Federation Identity Providers.

ACS can also be configured to support WS-Trust Identity Providers and OpenID-Based Identity Providers (using OpenID v2.0)[109]. ACS can also use OAuth to provide for federated authorisation[110].

The Force.com platform also supports federated authentication via the use of SAML. Any identity provider able to produce SAML v1.1 or v2.0 tokens (e.g. Microsoft's ADFS 2.0[111]) can be used to authenticate Force.com users. Consumers should be aware that this federated authentication via SAML is only available for controlling access to the Force.com website. SAML tokens cannot be used to authenticate to the web services API or the desktop client. Further information on the support (and implementation) of SAML-based federated authentication can be found at *http://wiki.developerforce.com/page/ Single_Sign-On_with_SAML_on_Force.com*.

---

[109] *http://msdn.microsoft.com/en-us/library/windowsazure/gg185971.aspx*.

[110] *http://msdn.microsoft.com/en-us/library/gg185937.aspx*.

[111] *http://wiki.developerforce.com/page/Single_Sign-On_with_Force.com_and_ Microsoft_Active_Directory_Federation_Services*.

A more complete guide to the implementation of single sign-on for Force.com applications can be found at *https://na1.salesforce.com/help/doc/en/salesforce_single_si gn_on.pdf*.

As well as OpenID, Force.com also supports OAuth v2.0 to allow federated authorisation of access to Force.com resources. Details of the OAuth support can be found at *http://wiki.developerforce.com/page/Digging_Deeper_into_ OAuth_2.0_on_Force.com*.

For those PaaS providers that provide less in the way of supporting security functionality within their platform – the Google App Engine and Heroku, for example – consumers must incorporate support for federated authentication and authorisation themselves (if required). The Spring Security framework incorporates support for OpenID and OAuth, and so may be a good basis for those PaaS consumers coding in Java.

Policy

The Policy service within the Access Management service grouping of the SRM delivers the information required by other services, such as Authenticate, Authorise and Filter. The Policy service dictates the access available to the relevant information resources. The Authenticate, Authorise and Filter services then use this information to determine whether or not to provide access.

The Access Management Policy service should be informed by the Policy service within the Security Management grouping (in turn taking a feed from the Compliance service), in order to ensure that access management decisions are taken in line with the business requirements.

In terms of Azure, for example, consumers need to develop a Policy service that is capable of processing the claims contained within the security tokens presented by the ACS, and deciding whether or not these claims are sufficient for access to be provided. At the Logical level, Policy services would typically comprise a Policy Information Point (containing the policy information) and a Policy Decision Point (which makes the access decision based upon the information within the PIP and the presented claims).

At the PaaS level, consumers have fewer policy decisions to worry about (or control, depending on your perspective) than at the IaaS level. PaaS consumers do not have the freedom to implement host-based or network-based COTS security products – such as firewalls, intrusion prevention systems, database firewalls, etc. and so they are reliant upon the policy decisions made by their PaaS provider[112].

Filter

The Filter service is responsible for enforcing the access decisions made elsewhere, e.g. by the Authorise service. The Filter service becomes more straightforward as you move through the Cloud service models (from IaaS through to SaaS), as the number of available logical and physical filters decreases. For example, whilst an IaaS consumer must (or at least should) concern themselves with filters at the network, operating system, database and application levels, consumers at the PaaS level need not concern themselves with the implementation of filters below their

---

[112] With the exception of the ability to control which IP address ranges (for example) may access their services or other host-based firewalling capabilities exposed by their CSP.

run-time. At least, in theory. In practice, things are a little more complicated.

Consider the mechanisms that consumers can use to connect to the PaaS. Whilst the most common scenarios for communication include the use of web portals and APIs, some PaaS CSPs will also offer more dedicated communications facilities, e.g. a capability to establish "private" encrypted links between your on-premise environment and the PaaS. Microsoft offers their Windows® Azure Connect service, which enables consumers to establish IPSec connections between on-premise machines and Azure roles. Azure Connect requires consumers to install a software agent on their on-premise machines in order to make use of the Connect service[113]. Connect enables consumers to configure Hybrid Cloud applications, e.g. a consumer could have their presentation servers sitting on Azure roles whilst the back-end databases remain on-premise with communications between the two protected by IPSec. Now, whilst the IPSec tunnels may act as an appropriate filter (via the establishment of cryptographic tunnels), with regard to ensuring the privacy of the communications between the on-premise machines and Azure, it does open up new risks. After all, there is now an encrypted connection between your on-premise and the Cloud; you have effectively extended your network into the Azure Cloud. The security of your on-premise machines is now dependent upon the filters implemented by Microsoft to prevent other Azure users (or Internet-based threats) from compromising the Azure roles hosting your applications. The other risk posed by such services is

---

[113] *http://msdn.microsoft.com/en-us/library/windowsazure/gg432997.aspx*.

related to illicit employee activity. Just because you can enable connectivity between your back-end databases and Cloud-based services does not mean that you should. The problem is in the encryption of the connections: how do you maintain control of the information flows, and ensure that information that should remain on-premise and protected does so? This brings me back to the point about consumers still needing to concern themselves about network filters even with PaaS solutions. Consumers must implement filters between their on-premise environment and the Cloud environment to ensure that only authorised information enters the Cloud.

Azure Connect is not the only service that poses the risk of unauthorised information leakage. The Azure Service Bus[114] enables Cloud consumers to easily integrate and orchestrate web services across the Cloud and on-premise environments. The Azure Service Bus is a great way to build mash-up applications consisting of capabilities provided by a variety of different web services. Consumers expose their internal web services to the Azure Service Bus, and the Service Bus then controls access to those exposed web services. Communications between the on-premise web services and the Service Bus are encrypted using SSL. However, as with Azure Connect, consumers become reliant upon the Cloud-based service (in this case, the Service Bus) to secure their on-premise web service. Again, as with Azure Connect, the communications between the back-end on-premise service and the Cloud is encrypted. A well-intentioned, but misinformed, employee could expose sensitive on-premise web services to the Cloud through

---

[114] *http://msdn.microsoft.com/en-us/library/windowsazure/ee732537.aspx*.

encrypted tunnels that are beneath the radar of your security team. This is another example of where consumers should consider implementing content-aware network level filters on-premise to manage issues relating to Cloud security.

When it comes to database and application level security filters (e.g. XML gateways and anti-malware services), PaaS consumers are limited in their options; COTS products providing such functionality cannot be installed on the Cloud. This is a strong disincentive for adopting the PaaS model if you are concerned about the protection of data and services held in the Cloud. There are alternative options – e.g. redirecting incoming requests or content to either on-premise or SaaS-based content-checking services – but these solutions will not always be ideal. XML Gateways (also known as "web services firewalls") can be used to control web services traffic flowing between the Cloud and on-premise environments, but such devices obviously have no visibility of communications flowing within a PaaS Cloud.

Within *Figure 9* (*Chapter 7*), I defined the Filter service as a joint responsibility in the PaaS delivery model. This is because PaaS consumers are reliant upon the separation mechanisms enforced by their CSPs to isolate their data and services from those of other PaaS consumers. Consumers should content themselves that the level of isolation is adequate to meet their needs. Different PaaS providers offer different levels of isolation, depending on their approach to delivering multi-tenancy.

For example, the Force.com platform approach to multi-tenancy is to offer a single database and infrastructure stack, and to separate organisations using a meta-data driven approach, as described at *www.developerforce.com/*

media/ForcedotcomBookLibrary/Force.com_Multitenancy_ WP_101508.pdf.

The Force.com platform can be viewed as a single, giant application, accompanied by a single, giant data store, with resources set aside for specific clients. The client-specific resources are identified by meta-data stored within the data store – for example, the Organisation ID (OrgID) can be used to scope which users can access resources specific to that organisation.

Conversely, the Heroku approach is based on the use of Linux Containers[115] to provide resource isolation for dynos, and the use of chroot (a facility common to most Unix-like operating systems) to provide file system isolation. Each dyno is, therefore, isolated from all other dynos. Windows® Azure offers isolation controls at the hypervisor and network levels. The Azure hypervisor prevents an Azure role operated by company A from being affected by the activities of an Azure role operated by company B on the same physical hardware. Azure also enforces network-level controls to ensure that customers can only access their own Azure roles. The Google App Engine runs each application within its own Sandbox[116], which strictly limits the interactions available to the application. For example, applications within the Sandbox cannot write to the local file system, open a network connection to another host directly, spawn sub-processes, or make system calls[117]. However, Google App Engine customers are utterly reliant on the strength of the Sandbox protecting their applications;

---

[115] *http://lxc.sourceforge.net/.*
[116] A sandbox is a mechanism for isolating and executing untrusted security programs.
[117] *http://code.google.com/appengine/docs/whatisgoogleappengine.html.*

delivery of this sandbox is completely in the domain of the CSP.

In summary, delivery of the Filter services must be through a combination of services delivered by the CSP and by the consumer. The consumer must understand the Filter services delivered by the CSP in order to identify any gaps in capabilities that they may need to address, or that will result in risks that must be managed (or simply accepted, based on an analysis of risk versus benefit).

Security Governance

The Security Governance services of the SRM are shown from a PaaS perspective in *Figure 27*.

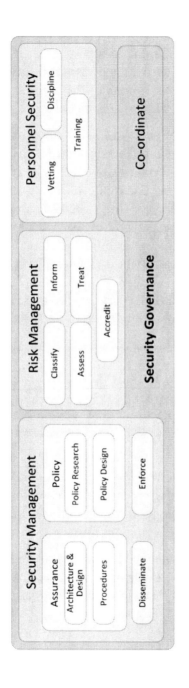

Figure 27: Illustrating the Security Governance services of the SRM

Yellow implies joint delivery responsibility. Green implies primary delivery responsibility sits with the consumer.

As you can see from *Figure 27*, all of the Security Governance services, with the exception of the Co-ordinate service, are now a joint delivery responsibility. The Co-ordinate service always remains the primary delivery responsibility of the consumer, as explained in *Chapter 8*.

The capabilities that the Security Governance services need to deliver are independent of the chosen IT delivery model. However, the delivery responsibility for the services varies across different Cloud service models. For example, whilst the Architecture & Design of a hosted application is primarily a consumer responsibility when deploying on an IaaS Cloud, it is a joint responsibility when deploying on a PaaS Cloud, and primarily the responsibility of the CSP when deploying on a SaaS Cloud. The capabilities associated with the individual services are described within *Chapter 9*; I will only describe (briefly) some PaaS-specific elements below.

Security Management

There is a joint responsibility to deliver the Security Management services of the SRM when working with PaaS.

Assurance, Architecture & Design, Procedures, Policy and Risk Management activities must be completed by the consumer (with respect to the application) and the CSP (with respect to the underlying platform and shared APIs).

Consumers must trust that such activities take place within their CSPs, preferably evidenced via certification to an international standard that demands such activities take place.

With regard to such services as Disseminate, consumers must ensure that they keep a close eye on the latest policy and procedural updates from their CSPs. These updates should then be further disseminated within the consumer to ensure that they feed into the application level aspects. Furthermore, these updates should also be compared against the consumer's underlying compliance and security policy requirements to ensure that the PaaS provider remains in a position to deliver these underlying requirements.

Security Operations

Security Operations is an area for which PaaS consumers can begin to realise some of the cost-savings associated with the Cloud. For example, as such consumers have no visibility of the operating system, they have no requirement to concern themselves with the patching of operating systems. This is the responsibility of the PaaS provider and is delivered as part of the Service within Platform as a Service. However, not all Security Operations are the responsibility of the PaaS provider. In fact, the majority of such services are a joint delivery responsibility in the PaaS model – as shown in *Figure 28*.

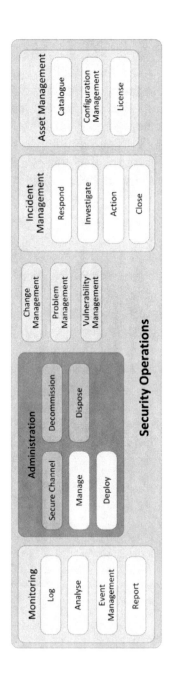

Figure 28: Illustrating the Security Operations services of the SRM

Yellow implies joint delivery responsibility. Red implies primary delivery responsibility sits with the CSP.

It is in the area of security operations that the need for joint delivery of security services becomes apparent. It is also the area where gaps are most likely to appear between the capabilities offered by the CSP and the capabilities implemented by the consumer. When I wrote, earlier in this book, that PaaS is the hardest of the Cloud service models to secure, it was primarily in the area of security operations that my concerns sat. Consumers must ensure that no gaps form between themselves and the CSP in such areas as Monitoring, Vulnerability Management and Incident Management.

Monitoring

The Monitoring service grouping of the SRM includes services to Log, Analyse and Report on security events alongside an Event Management service.

In the PaaS environment, it is the responsibility of the CSP to log events at the underlying network infrastructure and operating system level. Consumers must trust their CSPs to provide adequate security-monitoring capabilities alongside an Event Management process that will enable CSPs to inform their consumers of events requiring their attention and, more importantly, action.

It remains the responsibility of the consumer to instrument their application to provide the information required to meet both compliance requirements relating to audit and general security logging requirements. The Windows® Azure platform provides a specific API dedicated to monitoring and diagnostics[118]. *Table 4*[119] shows the information sources from which data can be collected.

Table 4: Azure Diagnostics

Data source	Description	Role types supported
Windows® Azure logs	Collected by default. Logs trace messages sent to the trace listener (added to the web.config or app.config file). For more information, see the DiagnosticMonitorTraceListener class.	Web and worker roles
IIS 7.0 logs	Collected by default. Logs information about IIS sites. For more information, see Configuring Logging in IIS 7. Note: IIS 7.0 logs are not collected for worker or VM roles, because worker and VM roles do not run within IIS.	Web roles only
Windows® Azure Diagnostic infrastructure logs	Collected by default. Logs information about the diagnostic infrastructure, the RemoteAccess module, and the RemoteForwarder module.	Web and worker roles

---

[118] *www.windowsazure.com/en-us/develop/net/common-tasks/diagnostics/*.
[119] Taken from *http://msdn.microsoft.com/en-us/library/windowsazure/hh411546.aspx*.

Failed Request logs	Logs information about failed requests to an IIS site or application.	Web roles only
Windows® Event logs	Logs events that are typically used for troubleshooting application and driver software.	Web and worker roles
Performance counters	Logs information about how well the operating system, application, or driver is performing.	Web and worker roles
Crash dumps	Logs information about the state of the operating system in the event of a system crash.	Web and worker roles
Custom error logs	By using local storage resources, custom data can be logged.	Web and worker roles

Users of this service must be aware that the collected information is transient, and so must be transferred across to more persistent storage (i.e. Azure Blob or Table storage) if the logs are to be preserved.

The Heroku PaaS also offers a specific logging capability (the Logplex), which enables consumers to obtain log information from their application, the Heroku platform (e.g. information on the restarting of crashed processes) and the Heroku management API (e.g. information on the deployment of new dynos, changes in scaling, etc.) The information held within the Logplex can be retrieved via the command line using the "heroku logs" command. More usefully, Heroku can also be configured to push the logs out to a syslog server defined by the consumer. Further information about the logging capabilities of Heroku can be found at *http://devcenter.heroku.com/articles/logging*.

Users of the Google App Engine must use the appropriate logging tools for their run-time of choice (e.g. Java or Python). Logs can then either be downloaded from the Administration Console or downloaded through the use of AppCfg[120] scripts.

Chapter 5 of the Force.com *Security Implementation Guide, 2012*[121] provides guidance on the comprehensive security auditing available within the Force.com platform. Force.com enables the auditing of user activities – e.g. logins and activities on data objects – such that a history of each object can be maintained. Logs can then be downloaded in either CSV or Gzip formats.

Now, given that CSPs tend to charge for storage and for data export per usage, there is a real incentive to ensure that you only log and then store information that is of real relevance. There is now a real cost driver to target your security logging, rather than log everything "just in case". Consumers should consider the activities and resources that are of most concern and target their logging at those activities. Consider the information likely to be of most value to an investigator – don't capture information that is likely to be of no value, unless there are compliance requirements demanding the capture of such information.

Logging is only the first part of the security monitoring process. Once the information has been captured, it must be

---

[120] Command line tool for interacting with the App Engine – *http://code.google.com/appengine/docs/appcfg.html*.
[121] *https://na1.salesforce.com/help/doc/en/salesforce_security_impl_guide.pdf*.

analysed. In most cases, I would recommend that PaaS consumers export the log information from the Cloud, and then pass that information across to whichever Security Event Management tool they currently use to deliver Analyse services (via an appropriate check for malicious content).

Following on from the Analyse service is the Event Management service. This, again, exposes a potential gap in delivery between the PaaS CSP and the consumer. Appropriate communication channels, including service-level agreements, must be in place to enable consumers and CSPs to exchange event information. Should a consumer identify a potentially suspicious event in the logs sourced from a CSP, they may require input from their CSP to decipher the exact meaning and implications of the audit entry. Failure to maintain an appropriate service level agreement may lead to excessive delays in the consumer obtaining the information that they require to act on a potential security event. Conversely, consumers must sustain an event management capability that CSPs can contact in the event of their own monitoring capabilities detecting an incident in progress at the consumer. Such an event management capability should also be responsible for monitoring the status websites of their various CSPs to ensure that consumers maintain awareness of system availability or wider security incidents. Examples of status update sites in the PaaS arena include:

- *http://trust.salesforce.com/trust/status/*
- *www.windowsazure.com/en-us/support/service-dashboard*
- *http://code.google.com/status/appengine*
- *http://status.heroku.com.*

If any information – be it from the application logs or from the CSP status updates – indicates a security incident, the Event Management service should initiate the Incident Management processes.

Administration

The Administration services of the SRM are as follows:

- Secure Channel
- Decommission
- Manage
- Dispose
- Deploy.

The Secure Channel, Decommission and Dispose services are clearly the primary delivery responsibilities of the CSP. The CSP provides the channels enabling the management of their platforms (usually via a web portal and an API). CSPs are also responsible for the decommissioning and subsequent disposal of the hardware providing the platform.

This leaves only the Manage and Deploy services as those over which the consumer has a degree of control. Even in a PaaS environment, consumers have a degree of control over their services – e.g. they can control the number of instances that they require to provide their services, the usage quotas that they require, etc. Consumers also decide when they deploy their applications to the PaaS platform. However, within the SRM, these services are marked as a joint delivery responsibility, given that the CSP provides the Manage and Deploy services with respect to the hardware, platform and shared APIs. Consumers should closely control the ability to manage and deploy their applications; not only could a rogue administrator delete (or stop) applications running in a PaaS environment, they could also attack their employers financially by running up excessive charges. Monitor your employees' management and deployment activities via the logs made available by your CSP.

Change Management and Problem Management

The Change and Problem Management services are, again, a joint delivery responsibility between the consumer and the CSP in a PaaS environment. A critical aspect of the Problem Management service is the identification of whether an issue resides with the CSP or with the consumer, and then managing that issue through to a successful resolution. As with some of the other SRM services, the success of this approach is dependent upon the consumer having a full understanding of the services provided by the CSP and appropriate communication channels being available.

In general, the consumer will be responsible for managing change and problems associated with their application. Issues can arise where problems are found in the platform APIs that are incorporated into a consumer application. Similarly, consumers must be aware of planned changes to such platform APIs, to ensure that they make the necessary changes to their application that is reliant upon the common functionality.

The PaaS approach can take care of some of the problems associated with change management – i.e. changes to the supporting infrastructure now take place "under the covers", and are no longer the concern of the consumer.

CSPs can also introduce new functionality that consumers can adopt in a managed fashion through scheduled change windows.

One downside of the PaaS approach is that change – and other maintenance – windows will occur at the choosing of the CSP, rather than that of any individual consumer. This can be a problem if a consumer has an important event occurring at the same time that the PaaS platform (or elements thereof) becomes unavailable.

Vulnerability Management

Vulnerability Management responsibilities are clearly split between the CSP and the consumer in the PaaS environment. The CSP must perform regular penetration tests and vulnerability assessments on their platform, whilst the consumer is responsible for the security of their application. However, the second part can be difficult to achieve, particularly if the PaaS provider does not allow penetration testing. Consumers should always contact their CSP prior to undertaking any penetration testing on the live platform, unless they have explicit authorisation to conduct such activities.

The area of Vulnerability Management highlights a clear disadvantage of the PaaS approach. With IaaS, consumers can run penetration testing exercises within the Cloud (by installing the necessary tools within their virtualised environments), but it is not possible to provide the same level of service within most PaaS environments. SaaS providers can test their services all the way up to the application level. With PaaS, whilst your CSP may scan and fix their platform on a regular basis (and most do[122]), you will still be in trouble if your own application hosts weaknesses that you are not allowed to identify.

The Force.com platform has found a novel way to support vulnerability assessment whilst maintaining control of the process. Firstly, they offer a source code scanner, which will identify problems at the source code level through static analysis of the provided code. Consumers upload their code to the URL below and are then presented with a report highlighting potential issues: *http://security.force.com/sourcescanner*.

The second facility provided by Force.com is a web application security assessment tool. Burp Suite® is a well-respected web application analysis tool commonly used by many penetration testing organisations. Force.com offers a free annual license to their customers. Force.com recommends that Burp be used where an application " … contains integrations with web services not residing on the Force.com Platform[123]". For those applications that reside on the Force.com platform, they recommend the use of the source code scanner referred to above. Further details of the Burp tool are provided by Force.com at *http://security.force.com/webappscannerdetails*.

Would-be users of the Burp tool should, however, also note the following text that appears on the page linked to above:

---

[122] See for example, *https://trust.salesforce.com/trust/security/*.
[123] *http://security.force.com/webappscanner*.

"Please note that you are not permitted to run this tool against any servers owned and operated by salesforce.com, without prior written approval."

Incident Management

Incident Management in the Cloud is another activity that demonstrates the need for comprehensive and timely communication channels between the CSP and the consumer. I strongly recommend that such communications channels are specified in contract terms, where there is the flexibility for consumers to negotiate. Consumers will likely require assistance from their CSPs (e.g. the provision of log information) to manage ongoing incidents. CSPs should also be able to provide extracts of secure logs that are suitable for use by law enforcement or in criminal trials, where necessary.

I provided extensive descriptions of incident response processes in *Chapter 9,* and so I will not repeat that content here.

Asset Management

Even in a PaaS environment, consumers must still maintain a catalogue of the assets that they have in the Cloud. This could relate to their roles in an Azure, dynos in a Heroku environment or data stored in any PaaS environment.

Consumers are also responsible for the configuration management of their PaaS applications – i.e. traditional source code management and deployment activities.

The issue of license management does not completely disappear in the Cloud, as certain services are licensed per user (e.g. Force.com), and so consumers must still ensure that they abide by their licensing agreements. Similarly, PaaS services also offer application stores where pre-built software applications for the platform can be purchased. Again, such applications will be subject to their own licensing terms and conditions.

Conclusion

This chapter has described some of the ways in which the SRM services can be delivered and some of the associated issues with regard to working in a PaaS environment. Many PaaS providers offer extensive documentation on the security of their services; I recommend that would-be consumers take a close look at such documentation prior to adopting such a service. Examples of the security documentation available can be found at:

- *http://wiki.developerforce.com/page/Security* (Force.com)
- *http://msdn.microsoft.com/en-us/library/windowsazure/ ff934690.aspx* (Windows® Azure).

CHAPTER 11: SECURITY AND SOFTWARE AS A SERVICE

In this chapter, I describe how the security services defined within the security reference model (SRM) – shown in *Figure 7* – may be delivered by consumers implementing a service using a Software as a Service (SaaS) Cloud.

The OpenCrowd taxonomy[124] of Cloud services splits SaaS CSPs into a number of different categories:

- Billing
- CRM
- Collaboration
- Content management
- Document management
- ERP
- Environmental health & safety
- Financials
- Health and wellness
- Human resources
- IT Services management
- Personal productivity
- Project management
- Sales
- Security
- Social networks.

---

[124] *http://cloudtaxonomy.opencrowd.com/taxonomy/platform-as-a-service/*.

Examples of SaaS providers include:

- Salesforce.com (*www.salesforce.com*)
- FinancialForce.com (*www.financialforce.com*)
- Sage (*www.sageone.com*)
- Intuit (*www.intuit.com*)
- Netsuite (*www.netsuite.com/portal/home.shtml*)
- SuccessFactors (*www.successfactors.com*)
- RightNow (*www.rightnow.com/cx-suite.php*)
- Oracle On Demand (*www.oracle.com/us/products/ ondemand/index.html*)
- Office 365 (*www.microsoft.com/en-gb/office365/online-software.aspx*)
- Google Apps (*www.google.com/apps/intl/en/business/ index.html*)
- Soho (*www.zoho.com*)
- Alfresco (*www.alfresco.com*)
- Yammer (*www.yammer.com*)
- Huddle (*www.huddle.com*)
- Box.net (*www.box.com*)
- DropBox (*www.dropbox.com/teams*)
- Qualys (*www.qualys.com*)
- MIMECast (*www.mimecast.com*)
- PingConnect (*www.pingidentity.com/our-solutions/ping connect.cfm*)
- MessageLabs (*www.symanteccloud.com/en/gb*).

Both the OpenCrowd taxonomy and the selection of SaaS CSPs given above highlight the real diversity that is present in the SaaS ecosystem. They also highlight the impossibility of providing detailed security guidance that is applicable to all categories of SaaS service provisions. The security requirements for a financial reporting system or a Human Resources (HR) system are clearly different from those for a system designed to promote collaboration, or a service providing security testing. The guidance presented in this chapter will necessarily be generic, and is aimed at helping organisations secure their use of services for which they entrust their data (and relying business processes) to SaaS vendors.

Secure Development

In a SaaS environment, the primary responsibility for the delivery of a secure application rests with the provider. SaaS providers should be extremely incentivised to provide a secure service; given the competitive nature of the SaaS landscape, a series of security mishaps will not be conducive to a long-term future.

One of the drivers for adopting the SaaS model is to rid yourself of the problem of software development and the overhead of supporting the developed software on an expensive infrastructure. However, the more complex the SaaS application, the more work is required to tailor it to meet your particular needs. Examples of the work involved can include "skinning" the application with your own logos and visual style guidelines, configuring the users and their access rights, transforming any data to be uploaded to the SaaS provider, and integrating the SaaS provider into your wider environment (e.g. implementing single sign-on). Deciding to adopt a SaaS model does not mean that you can immediately reassign your hands-on technical staff to other roles. You will need to retain some skilled resources to configure and then manage the technical or mundane administrative aspects of your chosen SaaS solution.

From a Secure Development perspective, then, whilst there will be little in the way of content, you will still require a limited set of Coding Standards (e.g. configuration guidelines), together with the capability to Code Review and Unit Test any preparatory work (e.g. upload scripts), prior to their usage. However, the bulk of the delivery responsibility for such services – in relation to the application itself – rests with the CSP.

Integrity

With a SaaS approach, you are buying into the integrity of the SaaS application and the underlying data stores. The only aspects of integrity that a consumer can influence relate to the integrity of the data provided to the CSP and the integrity of the organisation-specific configuration within the SaaS application. Consumers should also ensure that they maintain the integrity of their on-premise data stores by content-checking any information sourced from their SaaS provider prior to it being incorporated into a trusted data store.

From a Non-Repudiation perspective, SaaS consumers are limited to the audit functionality and non-repudiation capabilities offered by their SaaS provider. User activities on a SaaS application can only be captured by the provider, unless such activities are proxied between the consumer and the SaaS provider. Fortunately, such proxies do exist, and they can provide significantly more capability than simple logging of traffic between the on-premise environment and a SaaS provider.

XML security gateways – such as those from Vordel, Layer 7 and others discussed in previous chapters – can be used to sit between the on-premise environment and a SaaS provider, and inspect, log and secure communications with web services-based CSP APIs. Such products offer a more customisable source of audit and user activity information than may be available from your SaaS provider. These products can also handoff to anti-virus software to perform Content Checking duties in relation to attached or embedded files.

Dedicated Cloud security products, such as those from CipherCloud[125] and Perspecsys[126], can also be used to secure connections between consumers and their CSPs. These products offer some extremely valuable functionality with regard to the integrity of data and compliance with data residency requirements. Through either encryption or tokenisation, consumers can use these products to ensure that their sensitive data remains on-premise.

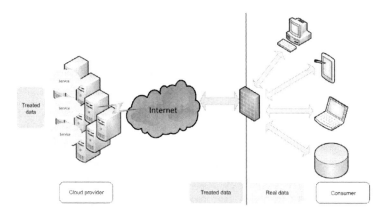

Figure 29: Use of a Cloud security gateway

The use of a Cloud security gateway enables consumers to keep their sensitive data on-premise, whilst still taking advantage of Cloud services.

---

[125] *www.ciphercloud.com/.*
[126] *www.perspecsys.com/.*

Figure 29 illustrates how such products work. On the left hand side we have our SaaS CSP, and on the right hand side we have our consumer on-premise environment. In this scenario, the consumer is keen to take full advantage of the functionality and flexibility offered by their CSP; however, they also have requirements to keep their sensitive data on-premise. The solution illustrated *in Figure 29* allows the consumer to meet both requirements. Users within the consuming organisation accessing their Cloud services, are unaware of the device sitting in between themselves and the SaaS provider. This device (e.g. a CipherCloud, Perspecsys, or other product) intercepts the sensitive data before it leaves the on-premise environment and replaces the sensitive data items with either encrypted or tokenised values. This treated data is then transmitted to the CSP and stored within the Cloud. When the user then needs to access the SaaS application, the SaaS application processes the treated data that it holds and returns the treated data to the end-user. Before the response reaches the end-user, the device replaces the treated data with the real data. End-users can, therefore, take full advantage of the capabilities of the SaaS application whilst retaining complete control of their sensitive data. In addition to the ability to keep data on-premise, such products also tend to offer the ability to control access to SaaS functionality and to maintain secure audit logs of activity on the SaaS service – acting as a SaaS application-level firewall, if you will. Such products require specific adapters to be able to integrate with different SaaS services; examples of SaaS services for which adapters are available include Google Apps, Salesforce.com and AWS[127].

---

[127] You should ensure that the product supports your chosen SaaS CSPs prior to purchase.

Implementing products, such as Perspecsys or CipherCloud, does have some downsides, however. For example:

- If their purpose is to keep data on-premise, then the devices must be implemented on-premise. Implementing new physical hardware may not be compatible with the aims of moving to Cloud-based delivery.
- Hardware and software does not maintain itself; the products will require configuration and maintenance, e.g. patching.
- These devices now act as a chokepoint for your SaaS access. Ensure that you can still meet required response times.
- These devices now become a single point of failure. You may need to install a high-availability or resilient pair, possibly at more than one location.

The above issues all point to significant financial investment (in terms of kit, hosting and management) – investment that may outweigh the financial benefit of moving to a pay-as-you-go model. Consumers should ensure that they factor all relevant issues into their cost/benefit analysis with regard to the adoption of SaaS if they have a requirement to keep their data on-premise.

The final service within the Integrity service grouping is the Snapshot service. In the IaaS and PaaS discussions, the Snapshot service was described as providing a known-good baseline of data, application or configuration information. In the SaaS environment, the Snapshot service could be implemented by exporting data at specific points, and then securely storing such data on-premise – e.g. through hashing and/or signing of the data export. SaaS providers may also offer their own, equivalent "snapshot" capability, although consumers would need to be comfortable with the verification of the snapshot data (e.g. signed hashing) and where it would be stored.

Availability

The options for Business Continuity and Disaster Recovery are limited in a SaaS environment. If an organisation has fully bought into the SaaS philosophy and has little in the way of on-premise equipment, data or technical IT expertise, then they will struggle to continue their business processes, should their SaaS fail. Furthermore, if a SaaS (or the CSP) fails catastrophically, consumers may also struggle to retrieve their data from the CSP. On the positive side, one of the selling points of the SaaS approach is the speed to operation – which is fast, compared with that for on-premise implementation. So, if there is a long-term outage, a consumer could simply switch providers – assuming that the consumer has access to the underlying business data. Obviously, such a supplier switchover would not be a trivial undertaking, and the feasibility of such an approach varies with the complexity of the service involved. It's also not just a technical issue – any switchover would also require users within the consuming organisation to be retrained to operate the new service and, potentially, changes to established business processes. So, whilst it may be a relatively trivial exercise to move from one Vulnerability Assessment as a Service provider to another (e.g. from Qualys to Plynt), it would be a much more painful exercise to switch your personal productivity suite from Google Apps to Office 365.

What concrete steps should a would-be SaaS consumer take to ensure that appropriate business continuity and disaster recovery mechanisms are in place?

1. Ensure that you know the availability requirements of the business processes relying on the proposed SaaS application.
2. Investigate whether your proposed SaaS CSP can meet the identified availability requirements before signing up, by examining published availability statistics.
3. Examine the recompense on offer from the CSP, should they fail to meet their published SLAs. Service credits may not be much comfort.
4. Consider the impact on your business processes, should the SaaS provider undergo outages of minutes, hours, days, or weeks. At which point (if any) is the outage unsustainable?
5. Consider storing a replicated copy of your business data either on-site or at a separate CSP to ensure that your data is always available, even if your SaaS application is not.
6. Plan for the worst-case scenario. If the SaaS is unavailable to the point of being unsustainable, what will you do? Options may include:
   o Fallback to a legacy on-premise system
   o Fallback to manual processes (making use of the copy of your business data)
   o Switching to an alternative SaaS solution
   o Nothing (if it's not a business-critical service).

The above steps are not intended to offer a comprehensive approach to business continuity; there are enough standards available – e.g. BS25999/ISO22301 – that provide detailed advice in this area. My aim is rather to suggest some questions that should be in the back of your mind as you plan a SaaS implementation. You should also consider the comparative cost of implementing similar levels of business continuity and disaster recovery using physical, on-premise, systems. Whilst the levels of BC/DR available in the SaaS world may be limited, the SaaS approach may still represent a more feasible or cost-effective solution, particularly where an organisation does not possess geographically distributed redundant data centres or has a poor track record of delivering available services.

As the Cloud model matures, a number of organisations are considering the delivery of complex business processes through a combination of many atomic Cloud services – sometimes integrated and managed via a service broker. For example, the implementation of separate sales, CRM, storage, and authentication SaaS services to deliver a single overall business process. This approach offers great flexibility, as you can switch in and out of different CSPs as new "best of breed" suppliers emerge – at least, in theory. In practice, life is made more difficult through the lack of common standards in the area of portability and interoperability. From an availability perspective, you can find the availability of your overall business process being less than you may imagine. Always remember that the availability of your overall business process is dependent upon the availability of each atomic service – i.e. failure at one element may take down the entire business process. A combination of four services offering 99.5% availability will only deliver a combined availability of 98%, which may not meet your needs. Of course, similar concerns affect systems hosted on-premise, where a failure of a critical server, database, switch, etc. could also adversely affect the availability of a service. Always remember to step back and consider the overall requirements for your business processes and the impacts of those requirements not being fulfilled, regardless of your proposed delivery approach.

Cryptography

The delivery of the services within the Cryptography grouping is firmly the responsibility of the SaaS CSP, in most instances. Only the SaaS CSP can define the encryption requirements needed to access their service, albeit that such access is usually protected via SSL. Furthermore, it is the responsibility of the CSP to properly implement any encryption (and associated key management) of customer data, should that be an element of their service. Given that the key management functions and the encryption implementation are both in the realm of the CSP, such a capability should not be viewed as offering protection from a threat actor within the CSP. The only choice available to the consumer in a vanilla SaaS implementation may be whether or not to enable encryption on their communications and data. However, remember that SaaS consumers can still choose to encrypt data on-premise, and only send encrypted data into the Cloud if they decide to implement products, such as those offered by CipherCloud.

Access Management

Unlike in the IaaS and PaaS chapters (*Chapters 9* and *10*), I am not, in this chapter, going to explore the individual access management facilities available within a variety of different SaaS providers. I will, instead, provide some generic guidance on how you can maintain control of your users and data when using SaaS providers.

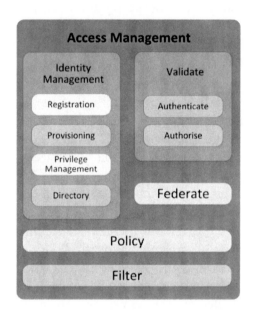

Figure 30: Illustrating the Access Management services of the SRM

Yellow implies joint delivery responsibility. Red implies primary delivery responsibility sits with the CSP.

Figure 30 shows the situation where you, as a SaaS consumer, adopt a standard implementation of a SaaS service. The CSP is responsible for how they authenticate your users to their service. The CSP is responsible for how they authorise access to your data and their functionality (on your data) within their application. The CSP provides the enforcement functionality (the Filter service) to enforce their access controls. All that's left for you, as a consumer, is to:

- Register your users.
- Assign the CSP's access rights.
- (Possibly) set an access management policy around access to the CSP's users – if such a capability exists.
- Decide whether or not to adopt federated identity management (if supported by the CSP).

Even those areas where the consumer still has some influence will be implemented using CSP-provided services – i.e. they remain a joint delivery responsibility.

For some consumers, this shifting of access management responsibilities may well count as one of the benefits of adopting a SaaS model. For others, it represents their worst nightmare of what can possibly go wrong with the Cloud model. As a SaaS consumer, you need to decide which camp you fall within; there is no generic right or wrong answer. Your answer should be the result of a consideration of the data concerned, the application concerned and the users concerned. The higher the risk associated with unauthorised access to your data, the more likely it is that you will not be content to delegate so much of the access management functionality to the CSP. So, what can you do if you are not content to rely solely upon your CSP?

I have mentioned XML gateways a number of times within this book. You may also see such products referred to as SOA firewalls. I'm essentially talking about such products as those from Vordel, Layer7 and Intel. As well as being able to parse XML, they also tend to support protocols, such as SAML and the eXtensible Access Control Markup

Language (XACML)[128]. XACML exists to provide a standard, extensible mechanism for describing and enforcing access control decisions. XACML allows organisations to externalise their authorisation decisions from their applications. In other words, applications will query an XACML-supporting Policy Decision Point (*see Figure 18, Chapter 9*) as to whether an access request should be allowed, rather than making the decision itself. XACML allows a centralised approach to authorisation across the application landscape. Of course, applications must be aware that they should be querying a PDP for their authorisation decisions in order for XACML to be effective. From a SaaS perspective, you may now be able to see how a combination of SAML and XACML can allow a centrally managed federated approach to authentication (via SAML) and authorisation (via XACML) to be achieved. By placing a gateway product that supports SAML and XACML between your on-premise environment and your SaaS providers, you can take back an element of control regarding *access management*. This scenario is illustrated in *Figure 31*.

---

[128] *www.oasis-open.org/committees/tc_home/php?wg_abbrev=xacml.*

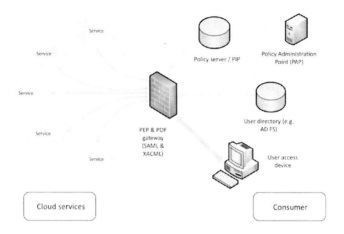

Figure 31: Demonstrating how the use of SAML and XACML can enable consumers to maintain control of authentication and authorisation whilst working with multiple SaaS CSPs

In *Figure 31*, all user access to a multitude of Cloud services is mediated via a gateway that supports SAML and XACML. This gateway interfaces with a user directory (such as Windows® ADFS) to enable federated authentication, and with a policy server to enable authorisation to the Cloud services via XACML. The Policy Administration Point is an XACML function used to manage the access policies held within the PIP. As with Cloud gateways, such as those from Layer 7 and Vordel (*see Chapter 10*), this approach does introduce a number of issues, including potential single points of failure in the form of the gateways themselves.

However, as we head towards a Cloud-based world, why limit yourself to on-premise hosted gateways? At RSA 2012, Intel announced their Intel Cloud SSO[129] service. This service enables single sign-on across hundreds of SaaS service – Identity Management as a Service, if you will. At launch, the Intel Cloud SSO includes connectors for SaaS products, including Google Apps, Office 365, Salesforce.com, SuccessFactors, WebEx®, Zoho and many more[130]. The Intel Cloud SSO is hosted on the Force.com platform and, so, is essentially a SaaS on a PaaS.

Other than maintaining a level of control over the delivery of Access Management services, an equally important result of adopting a single sign-on and control approach is user convenience. Consider a situation where a normal enterprise user must access applications hosted across their on-premise environment and across multiple SaaS providers. From a user experience perspective it is, undoubtedly, preferable to only authenticate once, and then be presented with access to all of your authorised applications – rather than be constantly prompted to enter your credentials.

Now, one danger of adopting an approach whereby you look to enforce control via some form of gateway is that you must ensure that your users actually traverse the gateway. This is easy enough when all of your users are based on-premise, but, more often than not, there will be a requirement to support mobile users, including users based on the Internet. In this scenario you must force your users to connect via your chosen gateway – e.g. by requiring your

---

[129] *www.intelcloudsso.com/* (the service is in Beta as of 3rd March, 2012).
[130] Taken from *http://info.intel.com/rs/intel/images/Cloud-SSO-Data-Sheet.pdf*.

remote users to connect to your on-premise network before hopping back to the Internet to access the SaaS services. You are also reliant upon your SaaS CSP to provide the functionality to limit the IP addresses from where users may connect to their service. If a user can go straight to the end point to access the application, why would they choose to go via the gateway?

So, to summarise:

• Help your users (and yourself) by implementing single sign-on.
• Make use of appropriate federation technologies based upon levels of risk, e.g. OpenID, OAuth, SAML, etc.
• Look towards XACML to externalise authorisation from your SaaS providers as support becomes more widespread.

Where you do not implement federated identity management, consider:

• Your authentication requirements (e.g. two-factor authentication) – can they be supported by your CSP?
• Your provisioning requirements – how straightforward is it to create users, distribute their credentials and remove or deactivate them, when necessary?
• Your authorisation requirements – are the levels of control within the application sufficiently granular? How straightforward is it to maintain user privileges?
• Your data privacy requirements – ensure you are legally entitled to populate SaaS-hosted user directories with the personal details of your employees (if relevant).

The Filter service is one that I will expand upon a little further. Although the SaaS provider is now completely responsible for the implementation of security enforcing functions within their application, consumers do sometimes still have a choice as to how they connect to their SaaS provider. For example, consumers should consider whether their CSPs offer the option of establishing dedicated encrypted connections into their services. As an example, Google Apps has the Secure Data Connector (SDC)[131], which encrypts traffic from the on-premise environment into the Google environment. The SDC also provides capabilities to limit the Google Apps functionality available to users within the consumer and so, in some ways, provides a similar set of services to those offered by more generic Cloud security or XML security gateways.

Another question that consumers should consider relates to the choice of Cloud deployment model. Some SaaS applications can be made available via a Public or Community Cloud model. This trend will increase, particularly where vendors are targeting Government clients; a number of SaaS CSPs are already offering Community Cloud services aimed at delivering to Government clients. Remember that "Cloud" must not always mean "Public Cloud".

Security Governance

The primary delivery responsibilities for the SRM Security Governance services for a SaaS application are shown in *Figure 32*.

---

[131] *http://developers.google.com/secure-data-connector/docs/1.3/overview.*

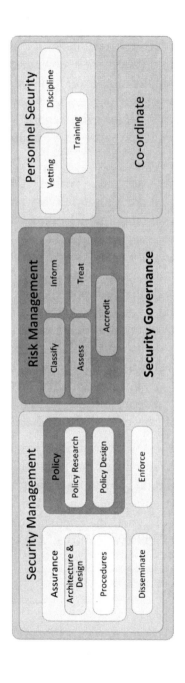

Figure 32: Illustrating the Security Governance services from the SRM

Yellow implies joint delivery responsibility. Red implies primary delivery responsibility sits with the CSP. Green indicates that primary delivery responsibility sits with the consumer.

The Risk Management responsibilities for the application are now the primary delivery responsibility of the SaaS provider; it is their application, and consumers have no control over how the application-level risks are managed. Consumers must, however, still remember to consider their risk management responsibilities with regard to their data and their business processes that rely upon the SaaS application.

There are still some services within the Security Governance grouping that are a joint delivery responsibility – for example, the Disseminate and Enforce services and the Personnel Security services. With regard to the Disseminate service, security policies and procedures must be disseminated to staff within both the CSP and the consumer. Similarly, both the CSP and the consumer must enforce those policies and procedures. In a SaaS environment, the CSP is primarily responsible for the delivery of a base set of security policies regarding how their service may be used. The consumer must provide their own set of policies and procedures for their own users, but the primary delivery responsibility for security policy regarding the SaaS application itself sits with the CSP.

The Personnel Security service grouping remains a joint delivery responsibility with SaaS, as it is with all Cloud models. Employees should be appropriately vetted and managed, whether they are employed by the CSP or the consumer; both sets of staff may pose a risk to the confidentiality, integrity and availability of the service.

Security Operations

The primary delivery responsibilities with respect to the SRM Security Operations services are shown in *Figure 33*.

In terms of the Administration services within the SRM, these services are, with the exception of Deploy, completely within the remit of the CSP. The CSP is responsible for the management of their service (e.g. security patching), provision of mechanisms to manage their service, and the subsequent decommissioning and disposal of their equipment upon failure or end of life. The one service within this grouping that is a joint delivery responsibility is the Deploy service. Even in a SaaS environment, consumers must still undertake a set of activities to deploy the application to their users, e.g. the provision of connectivity, access devices and user credentials, and the upload of business data and user training. It is these kinds of deployment activities that make Change Management a joint delivery responsibility. SaaS CSPs often tout their rolling programme of tightly managed application upgrades as a major advantage of the SaaS service model. SaaS consumers do not need to worry about keeping up to date with service patches or costly upgrades to the latest versions of their business applications – this is all part of the service in SaaS. However, such changes can have an impact on the business processes of the SaaS consumer. Consumers should, therefore, monitor CSP roadmaps to ensure that they are aware of upcoming functionality. This will ensure that consumers:

a) Take full advantage of new business opportunities that new functionality may offer.

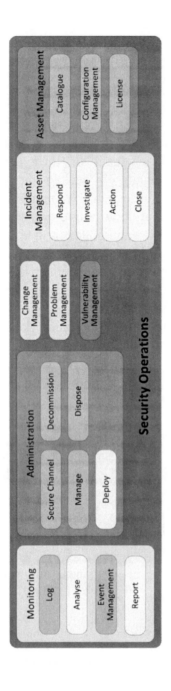

Figure 33: Illustrating the Security Operations services of the SRM

Yellow implies joint delivery responsibility. Red implies primary delivery responsibility sits with the CSP.

b) Do not suffer a sudden unexpected drop in availability, should a capability that their business users currently rely upon become deprecated in a scheduled update.

Problem Management is, similarly, a joint delivery responsibility; problems may arise from a misconfiguration of the application by the consumer, as well as from issues with the application or service itself. Communication channels must be available for each side to notify the other of potential issues with the service.

Vulnerability Management is firmly in the domain of the CSP in the SaaS environment; indeed, there would be little point in consumers performing security testing, as they would have no ability to fix any identified issues. Consumers should, instead, ensure that their CSPs have a thorough vulnerability management process in place, including regular penetration testing by qualified organisations.

The Incident Management services are a joint delivery responsibility; both consumers and CSPs must be able to respond to a security incident and, in some cases, respond jointly. As in other areas, where responsibility is joint (or where the CSP is primarily responsible), there must be a well-publicised communications facility available to, firstly, notify the other party of an incident, and then to enable both parties to manage the incident through to closure. SaaS consumers should be aware of the potential difficulties in obtaining evidence that is admissible in court from SaaS CSPs. However, as many organisations often choose to manage such incidents in-house – rather than involving law enforcement – so as to manage potentially adverse publicity, this may not be a major stumbling block.

The Asset Management services are primarily the responsibility of the CSP, as the CSP is responsible for the physical assets and software licenses providing their service. The consumer remains responsible for managing the licenses that may be associated with their usage of the SaaS application.

Conclusion

The SaaS service model is likely the most widely adopted of the Cloud service models, and is also the most diverse in terms of the services on offer. The SaaS CSPs are responsible for the delivery of a secure application, and there is little that a consumer can do to actively influence the security of the SaaS service. From an application perspective, consumers are often limited to controlling the data that they choose to upload to the CSP, configuring the access rights of their users, and monitoring the usage of the SaaS application. Consumers must also consider the security of the mechanisms that they use to connect their users and their data to the SaaS application, particularly as such communications tend to involve the Internet as the bearer. Do not forget that the fluffy Cloud terminology can often obscure the hard reality of the hostile Internet lurking underneath the surface.

Part Three: Conclusion

Part three presents a look ahead to the future of Cloud Computing and the likely impacts of future changes to the security of Cloud consumer data and services.

I then conclude with a summary and some closing thoughts on the security of Cloud Computing.

CHAPTER 12: LOOKING AHEAD

This book primarily concerns the current state of Cloud Computing. I believe an appropriate way to finish is to engage in a look to the near future of Cloud Computing and the attendant security implications. This chapter is purely my personal opinion on the likely evolution of Cloud Computing – you may well have different opinions!

Overview

I believe that Cloud Computing is here to stay; the agility and flexibility that Cloud offers cannot be matched by traditional delivery models. The increasing adoption of Cloud Computing by their clients will force the big systems integration companies to embrace the Cloud model. For the systems integration companies, this will mean:

- Offering their own Public Cloud services – be these IaaS, PaaS or SaaS.
- Becoming Cloud service brokers, stitching together individual Cloud offerings to provide a single business service (and contractual arrangement) to their clients[132].
- Offering business transformation services, helping their clients to take advantage of the Cloud approach.
- Building and/or hosting Private or Community Clouds on behalf of their clients.

---

[132] See *http://immediate.capgemini.com/*, for example.

Much of the above activity is already taking place. The unfortunate side effect (for their employees) will be an accompanying decline in the traditional outsourcing market and a shrinkage in the number of IT systems management roles related to outsourcing. In the short-term, I expect the major security impact to be one derived from ignorance. I expect organisations to accept too much risk, and/or the wrong type of risk, due to a lack of knowledge or understanding of Cloud security issues.

There is a view that the emergence of Cloud Computing will hasten the adoption of service-oriented architecture (SOA) amongst enterprises. This is a view that I share. SOA promotes loosely coupled services that work together to deliver business capability. This is a perfect fit with the model of using best-in-breed Cloud services to deliver a business capability. This is an area where systems integrators can continue to play a major role – acting as a Cloud service broker identifying the best-in-breed services, and stitching the individual services into a cohesive business capability that they can then present to their clients. Alternatively, end-user organisations could perform this role themselves, but would then need to assume the duties of due diligence and contract management with a multitude of different CSPs, rather than with a single Cloud broker. The security implications of stitching many different Cloud services are numerous – but manageable, if done correctly. Examples of the types of security questions that may arise when using a multitude of Cloud services include:

- Modelling of data flows: how does the data move between the different CSPs? Where does that data reside? How can data be deleted or extracted, if required?

- Modelling of service levels: are the service levels of the different CSPs compatible? If one CSP requires an interface to be up 99.99% of the time, and the CSP providing that interface only offers 99.5% availability, can you manage the difference?
- How straightforward is it to replace CSPs when another CSP assumes the best-in-breed position?
- Can you provide single sign-on across your entire Cloud ecosystem?
- Can you provide consistent and cohesive security monitoring across your entire Cloud ecosystem? For example, can you have a single identity across all parties?
- Can you have consistent and cohesive authorisation across the ecosystem? If an activity is barred on one CSP, should it be allowed on another, if that CSP cannot support the same granularity of access control?

Again, some would say that the above issues are already being wrestled with in a number of organisations. I would agree with that perspective. However, this use of the diverse Cloud ecosystem is not yet common, and so I feel justified in saying that such issues will become more apparent in the near future. The impact of such issues may well be more severe for those organisations that have adopted Cloud piecemeal, and have done so without consulting their IT departments.

From an end-user organisation perspective, the Cloud (in the widest sense) will continue to have a major impact on working practices. More and more ICT users will spend most of their working hours on the Internet, accessing support services and business applications that are hosted within the Cloud. There will be an increasing adoption of "Bring your own Device" (BYOD), whereby organisations provide their staff with an allowance to purchase their own preferred IT equipment, rather than managing a central pool of standardised equipment. Cloud is a great leveller in terms of its ubiquitous support for a multitude of different client access devices, such as laptops, mobile phones and tablets. Remember, all that is needed to access a large number of Cloud services is a browser, an Internet connection and an appropriate set of access credentials. The security implications here are interesting:

- You can't trust the network bearer (the Internet); all sensitive traffic should be encrypted.
- There is no device standardisation; you cannot trust the endpoint. and so manage content delivery appropriately – for example, you cannot keep the data within the Cloud.
- As you cannot trust the end point – or the network – you must ensure that your user authentication mechanisms are suitably robust.

An increasing number of organisations will adopt data-centric access controls and federated identity management to promote collaboration with their partners. In this latter scenario, doesn't it make more sense for these federated identities and shared data to reside within the Cloud – alongside their partners – rather than locked away behind leaky firewalls? There may even be an increased use of OpenID-style authentication for business purposes, where there is a low level of risk. This leads on to a gradual merging of social and business identities, whereby individuals can log on to low-risk business services using their Facebook, Gmail, Windows® Live or any other identities. Individuals may decide to formalise their holding of multiple identities. We all have multiple identities at the moment, whether we choose to recognise it or not; we have our work identities (usernames, payroll numbers, etc.), we have our financial identities (bank account details, credit card numbers), and we have our social identities (Facebook IDs, e-mail addresses, etc.) Wouldn't it be good to be able to use these identities as we see fit, rather than having to provide the same information to a multitude of organisations? Oftentimes it is a user's entitlement to access data or a service that is of importance to a business, rather than their actual identity; users could choose to use different identity and attribute providers to hold different personal details. They could then use OpenID and OAuth to only provide the personal information they are comfortable with sharing with the relevant party – be that their employer, their bank or their government. Whilst this may seem a little far-fetched, I should note that the UK Government are currently attempting to create a market in identity providers under their Citizen Identity Assurance Programme[133]. If such a market can be successfully established, then the idea of individuals using different identities for different purposes, in a more formal and educated manner than is currently the case, becomes less farfetched. From a security perspective, there are issues with this approach:

- Which identity providers do you trust?
- How do you verify that the identity providers operate as they claim?

---

[133] *http://digital.cabinetoffice.gov.uk/2012/03/01/identity-a-small-step/.*

- How do you know how strongly verified a user identity was at the point of registration?
- If you are only using attributes, rather than identities, how do you track transactions? Do you need to track all transactions?

So far, I've outlined a fairly rosy view of the future – one in which empowered users get to work in a flexible, collaborative environment empowered by the Cloud. It's a future in which businesses benefit from lower costs of operation, easier collaboration with their partners, more intimacy with their clients and more resources to allocate to improving their business, rather than looking after their IT. However, I don't expect everything to be so straightforward. I expect that, within the next two years, at least one major Cloud provider will see their management systems hacked – granting unauthorised access to their customers' data – and have this event publically exposed. This will, again, raise the question of the security of the Cloud model. Commentators will, again, forget quite how many on-premise IT systems are currently hacked on a daily basis. My advice is to expect such a hack to take place, and to design your services and business processes to be able to cope with such an event for when it does.

My other major concern with the Cloud model relates to data privacy and wider regulatory issues. The European Union has recently released a set of proposals to modernise existing European data protection legislation[134]. The proposals include some changes that would have a direct

---

[134] *http://europa.eu/rapid/pressReleasesAction.do?reference=IP/12/46.*

impact on the use of Cloud Computing. For example, there is a requirement that EU rules must apply if personal data is handled outside of the EU by companies that offer their services to EU citizens. Another potential difficulty relates to the proposed "right to be forgotten", whereby an individual should be able to force organisations to delete their information once there are no legitimate grounds for it to be retained. Now, there is no guarantee that the proposals mentioned above shall be accepted; however, it is indicative of the preferred direction of travel of the EU. The issue that I see is not one of data protection legislation being too strict, or too lax, but that it is too different across the globe. A Cloud service that is acceptable in one jurisdiction may be illegal in another. That same service may actually have been legal if it has been hosted within the relevant jurisdiction – i.e. it is only illegal because it is not within the same jurisdiction; consider the transfer of personal data outside of the European Economic Area, for example. There are also concerns regarding the use of Cloud services hosted within repressive regimes, or within regimes that are viewed with suspicion by other national governments. Unless mechanisms can be agreed and implemented to standardise upon regulatory requirements, the Cloud model could well fracture, rather than be global in nature. This will have negative consequences for the scale – and so too the volume-driven prices – that CSPs will be able to offer. In addition, as the broker model of delivering capabilities matures, organisations are going to have to take even more careful account of their supply chain to ensure that they are content with the base location of all of their suppliers.

But I do not want to end this chapter on a negative note. I feel that the Cloud model offers unprecedented opportunities for enterprises to refocus on their core business activities, rather than their IT operations. Business stakeholders are no longer beholden to IT departments to provide them with IT services. The move to Cloud will be accompanied by security professionals increasingly accepting the need to tolerate risk, in order to increase benefit and to retain their own relevance (and employment). The role of the security professional will morph, over the next few years, into that of someone able to:

- Accurately describe risk in business terms.
- Put forward pragmatic solutions to manage identified risks.
- Recognise that it's no longer acceptable to just say, "No" to risks that they don't understand.

My predictions may be wrong, and the Cloud may burst like other bubbles before it. However, I believe that the current economic uncertainties will sustain the Cloud model for the foreseeable future. There will be little cash available within the Government or enterprises for major capital expenditure in IT infrastructure for a number of years yet. Businesses will not stand still during this time, and so must adopt new ways of working. The future for Cloud Computing, at least, looks bright.

CHAPTER 13: CONCLUSION AND SUMMARY

The purpose of this book has been to act as a guide to the possibilities open to those looking to adopt Cloud Computing in a risk-managed manner. In order to do so, I've adopted a fairly standard format: an introduction to the problem space, a review of past work, a suggested approach, and then examples of how that approach can be implemented.

I have not tried to be exhaustive, overly comprehensive or dictatorial in tone. My aim has been to suggest an approach and a set of controls for your consideration; only you, your business stakeholders and security subject matter experts can decide which controls are appropriate for your particular application or service. I view this book as being something akin to a travel guide; I have suggested areas that may be of interest, but it is up to you to define your own itinerary based upon your own needs! Alternatively, but still on a geographical theme, you could also view this book as a map – but certainly not as a set of directions. In summary, stripping out the technical content, the advice within this book can be condensed down to the following guidance:

1. Gather your requirements: business and non-functional.
2. Perform a risk assessment.
3. Use your requirements and the outputs from your risk assessment to derive a set of conceptual services.
4. Consider how you can deliver these conceptual services at the Logical and Physical level using your chosen Cloud delivery approach.

5. If you cannot deliver a conceptual service, then re-examine the underlying requirements and risks; if a requirement can be refined to a more deliverable form, then do so (in agreement with the relevant stakeholders).
6. Collate any undeliverable services and unmitigated risks into a document explaining the attendant potential business impacts.
7. Obtain business sign-off from a responsible stakeholder to confirm that they fully understand, and accept, the residual risks.
8. Build and deploy your application, maintaining traceability back to the conceptual services, and so to the underlying requirements and risks.
9. Build governance processes to maintain the architecture during the system life cycle: change management processes, continuing requirements analysis, regular security assessments, etc.

Does the above approach guarantee a 100% secure Cloud application? Of course not, as there's no such thing as 100% secure (which is, itself, a fairly meaningless term). However, what this approach does provide is a mutual understanding between all parties within the consumer of the level of risk associated with a Cloud deployment. The relevant stakeholders can then decide if that level of risk is acceptable when balanced against a perceived business benefit. Always remember that it is the role of the business to decide whether a risk is acceptable; it is the role of the security professional to ensure that the business takes such decisions from an informed position.

I hope that my view on the security of Cloud Computing has become apparent over the course of the last couple of hundred pages. However, if not, I'll conclude this book with a series of bullet points to highlight some key messages:

- Cloud Computing is an evolution, not a revolution, in terms of the delivery of information systems.
- Cloud Computing has the potential to be a revolution, not just an evolution, in terms of the business approach to, and use of, information systems.
- Cloud Computing increases the attack surface of applications and services; multi-tenancy can occur at any level of the technology stack, but wherever it occurs, there's a boundary between your service and something else that would not be present in a siloed on-premise implementation.
- Cloud Computing can be secured to a level appropriate to the business requirements of most, but not all, organisations.
- The Public Cloud is not the only Cloud. Community and Private Clouds have their own valid use cases, particularly for those with strong compliance or assurance requirements.
- Security architecture methodologies should be used to link the business requirements, appetite for risk and compliance requirements to the delivery of security services.
- Traceability is important – you must be able to demonstrate why a security control is in place, the risks it mitigates and/or the business requirement(s) it delivers.
- The primary delivery responsibility for security services shifts from the consumer to the CSP as you move from

IaaS to SaaS. This can be a good thing or a bad thing, depending on your existing in-house security capabilities.

- PaaS is often the most troublesome service model to secure, due to the high number of services that must be delivered by both the consumer and the CSP; gaps are likely to appear between the two, unless very carefully managed.
- Cloud services will get hacked, and possibly even completely and utterly compromised. The same could be said for your on-premise equipment or your existing technology providers. Factor the risk of Cloud compromise into your decision-making process. Supply chain compromise is not a new issue – just a very difficult one to resolve.
- The business benefits that Cloud offers in terms of moving IT departments "out of the way" of business delivery, increases in agility, elasticity, mobility and collaboration means that it is here to stay; security professionals must either adopt a pragmatic mindset or prepare for retirement.
- "Secure" means delivering services that do not exceed the risk appetite set by the business. It does not mean delivering 99.99% hacker-proof (but unusable) services.

And, finally, it's time for informed risk management and not ignorant risk avoidance. I hope I have helped to inform. Good luck!

APPENDIX A: SRM SECURITY SERVICE ASSIGNMENTS

Service Name	Level	IaaS Rationale	PaaS Rationale	SaaS Rationale
Secure Development	0	Consumers are responsible for the security of any in-house developed applications that they host on an IaaS Cloud.	A PaaS will typically include a set of provided APIs for use by the consumer. The provider is responsible for the secure development of those APIs; the consumer is responsible for the security development of applications making use of those APIs.	The SaaS provider is responsible for the delivery of a secure application.
Coding Standards	1		The consumer must implement a set of coding standards to ensure that they use the provider's APIs correctly. The provider must implement a set of coding standards to ensure that they code secure APIs for use by their consumers.	
Code Review	1			
Unit Test	1			

Appendix A: SRM Security Service Assignments

Integrity	0	Consumers are responsible for building any integrity checking mechanisms into the services they host on an IaaS Cloud.	The provider is responsible for the integrity of the operating system and any provided APIs. The consumer is responsible for the integrity of the hosted application.	The provider is responsible for the integrity of the data that they host and the service(s) that they offer.
Non-Repudiation	1			
Content Check	1			Depending on the nature of the SaaS, consumers may be required to set up data validation rules.
Snapshot	1			
Hosting	0	The provider is responsible for the physical hosting of their service.	The provider is responsible for the physical hosting of their service.	The provider is responsible for the physical hosting of their service.
Physical Security	1			

Environmental Security	1			
Storage	1			
Communications	1			
Compliance	0	The risks (and penalties) associated with breaches of compliance cannot be outsourced. Whilst the compliance status of the provider can be helpful, the primary responsibility for compliance remains with the consumer.	The risks (and penalties) associated with breaches of compliance cannot be outsourced. Whilst the compliance status of the provider can be helpful, the primary responsibility for compliance remains with the consumer.	The risks (and penalties) associated with breaches of compliance cannot be outsourced. Whilst the compliance status of the provider can be helpful, the primary responsibility for compliance remains with the consumer.
Audit	1			
Test	1			
Regime	1			
Identify	2			

Appendix A: SRM Security Service Assignments

Translate	2			
Availability	0	The responsibility for delivering availability requirements is shared between the consumer and the provider. The provider must provide a resilient service; the consumer must build a resilient application upon that service.	The responsibility for delivering availability requirements is shared between the consumer and the provider. The provider must provide a resilient service; the consumer must build a resilient application upon that service.	The responsibility for delivering availability requirements is shared between the consumer and the provider. The provider must provide a resilient service; the consumer must build appropriate business continuity processes to ensure that it can survive any outages at the provider.
Business Continuity (BC)	1	The consumer must ensure that its critical business processes can continue in the event of the application failing.	The consumer must ensure that its critical business processes can continue in the event of the application failing.	The consumer must ensure that its critical business processes can continue in the event of the application failing.
BC Planning	2			
BC Implement	2			
BC Test	2			

Backup	1	The consumer is responsible for ensuring that the application and associated data is backed up, so as to be available in the event of failure.	The consumer should ensure that critical data is backed up; this may be on-premise or at an alternative provider. Depending on the scope of the platform, the provider may be responsible for back-up of the application data.	The consumer should ensure that critical data is backed up; this may be on-premise or at an alternative provider. The provider is responsible for the secure back-up of the application data of their consumers.
Failover	1	Failover is a joint delivery responsibility. The consumer must design their services such that they can failover effectively – either within different containers (e.g. AWS Regions or Availability Zones), within a single IaaS or, alternatively, across different IaaS Clouds. The provider must ensure that hardware failures are transparent to their consumers.	The consumer must code their application so as to take advantage of the failover capabilities of the Cloud platform. The provider must ensure that their services failover gracefully in the event of system or application fault.	The provider must ensure that their services failover gracefully in the event of system or application fault. The consumer remains responsible for ensuring that their connectivity to their provider can failover gracefully in the event of hardware or ISP failure.

Disaster Recovery (DR)	1	Disaster Recovery is a joint responsibility. The provider is responsible for ensuring that any hardware or data centre failure can be recovered. The consumer is responsible for designing their service such that it can be recovered in similar circumstances.	Disaster Recovery is a joint responsibility. The provider is responsible for ensuring that any hardware, data centre failure or shared service failure can be recovered. The consumer is responsible for designing their service such that it can be recovered in similar circumstances.	Disaster Recovery is a joint responsibility. The provider is responsible for ensuring that any hardware, data centre or application failure can be recovered. The consumer is responsible for ensuring that their service can be recovered in the event of a DR invocation.
DR Planning	2			
DR Implement	2			
DR Test	2			
Cryptography	0	The consumer retains primary delivery responsibility for Cryptography services – e.g. data encryption and encryption of traffic between end-users and the hosted application.	The consumer is responsible for the appropriate use of the Cryptography services provided by the platform. The consumer can also develop their own Cryptographic services to run on the platform. The provider is responsible for the delivery of the Cryptographic services they offer.	The provider now has primary responsibility for the implementation of Cryptographic services. The consumer retains responsibility for ensuring the security of the keys and certificates used to access the SaaS.

Encryption	1	The consumer is responsible for the design and implementation of Cncryption services from the operating system upward. This includes the use of encrypted network protocols within their virtual environment. The provider is only responsible for the provision of the encrypted channel used to administer the service.	The consumer is responsible for the appropriate use of the Cryptography services provided by the platform. The consumer can also develop their own Cryptographic services to run on the platform. The provider is responsible for the delivery of the Cryptographic services they offer.	The provider is responsible for the design and implementation of encryption at network and data levels. The consumer can (typically) only decide whether to access the service using http or https.
Key Management	1	Key management is primarily the responsibility of the consumer.	Key management can be a joint responsibility in a PaaS – e.g. where keys or certificates are imported into authentication and authorisation services offered by the provider.	Key management remains a joint responsibility in a SaaS environment, as the consumer retains responsibility for the secure management of the certificates used to access the service.

Access Management	0	The consumer is responsible for the access management relating to the hosted application. (The provider secures access to the IaaS administration features.)	Many platforms provide Access Management services. The provider is responsible for the security of these Access Management services. The consumer is responsible for the secure use of these services. Consumers can also develop their own Access Management services.	The provider is responsible for the provision of the Access Management services. The consumer is limited to the use of the Access Management services, e.g. deciding which roles should be assigned to their users.
Identity Management	1	The consumer is responsible for designing and implementing the Identity Management services used by their application.	The consumer may be responsible for the development of the Identity Management services used by their application. The consumer may choose to make use of shared Identity Management services provided by the PaaS. The provider is responsible for the security of the Identity Management services that they offer.	The provider has primary responsibility for the provision of the Identity Management services. The consumer will typically only make use of the services made available by their provider.
Registration	2		The consumer is responsible for ensuring that they have a suitable user registration process. This may involve usage of services provided by the PaaS.	The consumer is responsible for ensuring that they have a suitable user registration process. Users must be registered in the SaaS, or the SaaS must be configured to make use of federated identity management.

Provisioning	2	Application users will be provisioned using mechanisms under the control of the consumer.	Depending on the application, users may be provisioned independently of the Cloud provider. More likely, application users will be configured using APIs provided by the Cloud provider.	Application users are provisioned using the tools provided by the SaaS provider. (Provisioning is, essentially, a technical service unlike Registration)
Privilege Management	2			
Directory	2			The user directory is provided by the SaaS provider.
Validate	1	The consumer is responsible for the delivery of the Validation services – e.g. the delivery of application authentication mechanisms.	The provider offers authentication and authorisation APIs that should be reused by the consumer. The provider is, therefore, primarily responsible for the delivery of these services.	The shared application includes the Validate services.
Authenticate	2	The consumer decides upon (and then implements) the authentication mechanisms used by their application.	The consumer will usually make use of the Authentication services delivered by the provider.	The consumer must make use of the authentication mechanisms supported by the shared application.

Authorise	2	The consumer decides upon (and then implements) the authorisation mechanisms used by their application.	The consumer will usually make use of the Authorisation services delivered by the provider.	The consumer must make use of the authorisation mechanisms supported by the shared application.
Federate	1	The consumer is responsible for any Federation mechanisms, e.g. the establishment of trust frameworks.	The consumer has primary responsibility for any Federation mechanisms, e.g. the establishment of trust frameworks.	The consumer has primary responsibility for any Federation mechanisms, e.g. the establishment of trust frameworks. The provider's application must be able to support federation.
Policy (AM)	1	The consumer sets the access management policy for the hosted service.	The consumer sets the access management policy for the application. The provider sets the access management policy for the shared APIs.	The provider sets the overall access management policy for the service. The consumer may set the specific access management policy for their implementation.
Filter	1	Delivery of the Filter service is a joint responsibility. The provider is responsible for the provision of Filter capabilities with respect to the underlying IaaS. The consumer is	Delivery of the Filter service is a joint responsibility. The provider is responsible for the provision of Filter capabilities with respect to the underlying PaaS. The consumer is responsible for Filter services protecting the hosted application.	The provider is responsible for the Filter services protecting the shared application.

Security Governance 0	responsible for Filter services protecting the hosted application. • The consumer must provide the security governance frameworks under which the hosted application is delivered and operated.	• The consumer and provider must jointly provide the security governance frameworks under which the hosted application is delivered and operated.	• The consumer and provider must jointly provide the security governance frameworks under which the shared application is delivered and used.
• Security Management • 1	• The consumer must design the technical architecture and operating procedures for the hosted application; this includes the associated security management capabilities.	• The consumer must design the technical architecture and operating procedures for the hosted application. The provider must do likewise for the shared services.	• The consumer must design the operating procedures for their use of the hosted application. The provider must provide the security management for the hosted application.
• Assurance • 2			
Architecture & 3	The consumer is responsible for the	The provider is responsible for the architecture and design of the shared	The provider is responsible for the architecture and

Service				
Design		architecture and design of their application and its hosting environment. The provider is responsible only for the design of the underlying hardware.	services. The consumer is responsible for the architecture and design of the hosted application itself.	design of the service. The consumer may be responsible for small levels of customisation, e.g. "skinning" the application through the use of corporate colours and logos.
Procedures	3			
Policy (SM)	2	The consumer is responsible for the production of the security policies relating to the hosted application.	The provider is responsible for setting the security management policies for the usage of their shared services. The consumer is responsible for the security management policies for how those shared services are to be used and how the application itself must be used.	The provider is responsible for the top-level security management policy of the application. The consumer can only set policies governing their usage of the application.
Policy Research	3			
Policy Design	3			
Disseminate	2	Dissemination of security policy regarding the application is primarily the responsibility of the	Dissemination of security policy is a joint responsibility; both the consumer and provider must disseminate the security policy to	Dissemination is a joint responsibility; both the consumer and provider must disseminate the security policy to their respective

		consumer.	their respective users.	users.
Enforce	2			
Risk Management	1	The consumer remains responsible for ensuring that risks to the application are identified and appropriately managed.	The consumer must ensure that risks to their own application are identified and managed. The provider must ensure that risks to their shared APIs are identified and managed.	The provider is responsible for ensuring that risks to the application are identified and appropriately managed. The consumer may wish to assure itself that the provider is managing risk appropriately.
Classify	2			
Inform	2			
Assess	2			
Treat	2			
Accredit	2			
Personnel Security	1	Personnel Security is a joint responsibility – the consumer is responsible for the Vetting, Discipline and Training of their end-users and administrative staff; the provider is likewise responsible for their own	Personnel Security is a joint responsibility – the consumer is responsible for the Vetting, Discipline and Training of their end-users and administrative staff; the provider is likewise responsible for their own staff.	Personnel Security is a joint responsibility – the consumer is responsible for the Vetting, Discipline and Training of their end-users and administrative staff; the provider is likewise

Appendix A: SRM Security Service Assignments

		staff.		responsible for their own staff.
Vetting	2			
Discipline	2			
Training	2			
Co-ordinate	1	It is the responsibility of the consumer to co-ordinate all aspects of their service.	It is the responsibility of the consumer to co-ordinate all aspects of the security of their service.	It is the responsibility of the consumer to co-ordinate all aspects of the security of their service.
Security Operations	0	Security Operations remains primarily the responsibility of the consumer, although the provider must play its part.	The provider is responsible for security operations up to and including the operating system layer. The consumer is responsible for security operations at the application level (with the exception of the shared APIs)	The provider is responsible for security operations up to and including the application. The consumer may choose to implement some Security Operations services on-premise.
Monitoring	1	The consumer is responsible for the security monitoring of the hosted application; the provider is responsible for the monitoring of the	The consumer is responsible for the security monitoring of the hosted application. The provider is responsible for monitoring of the underlying hardware, and also of the shared services (e.g. authentication	The consumer is responsible for the monitoring of the use of the application by their end-users. The provider is responsible for the monitoring of the

		underlying IaaS. For example, the provider must be able to recognise distributed denial-of-service attacks against its service.	and authorisation).	security of the application and the supporting platform.
Log	2	The consumer must decide which (virtual) network, operating system and application level events they wish to capture.	The consumer must decide which events their application must log.	The provider is responsible for deciding which events the application can log. The consumer may have some flexibility over which of these events they choose to log.
Analyse	2	The consumer must put in place the capability to analyse security logs.	The analysis tasks are split across the consumer and the provider. Both parties must implement analysis capabilities.	The analysis tasks are split across the consumer and the provider. Both parties must implement analysis capabilities.
Event Management	2	The consumer has the access to manage most events, with the exception of hardware and physical network issues.	Events affecting shared services must be jointly managed, e.g. to ascertain whether there is a problem with the shared service itself or simply with the implementation of the shared service by the application itself.	Events affecting the application as a whole, or the underlying platform, must be managed by the provider. Traditional misuse of authorised access by end-users must still involve the

				consumer.
Report	2	The consumer has access to most of the information required to Report on security events.	The consumer must work with the reporting services offered by the provider to gather the necessary information to produce the Report.	The consumer must work with the services offered by the provider to gather necessary information to produce the Report.
Administration	1	The consumer is responsible for the administration of all aspects of the hosted application, from the operating system upwards.	The provider is responsible for the administration of everything other than the application itself.	The provider is responsible for all system administration.
Secure Channel	2	The consumer must decide on appropriate management channels within their virtualised environment.	The provider must ensure that appropriate out-of-band management channels are used.	The provider must ensure that appropriate out-of-band management channels are used.
Decommission	2	Decommissioning is a joint responsibility – the consumer must de-commission its hosted services, whilst the provider must make sure that released resources	Decommissioning is primarily the responsibility of the provider; both virtual images and physical hardware are within their scope of provision.	Decommissioning is the responsibility of the provider.

		do not expose consumer data to other users of the IaaS.		The provider is responsible for all management of the service (with the exception of any user-configurable elements, such as "skinning").
Manage	2	The consumer is responsible for the management of their virtual environment from the network upwards.	The provider is responsible for server management and the management of any shared services. The consumer is responsible for application management.	
Dispose	2	The provider is responsible for the secure disposal of decommissioned hardware.	The provider is responsible for the secure disposal of decommissioned hardware.	The provider is responsible for the secure disposal of decommissioned hardware.
Deploy	2			
Change Management	1	The consumer retains primary responsibility for managing change to the hosted application and the supporting operating system.	The consumer retains responsibility for managing change to the application, but this must be in consideration of changes to any shared services. The provider is responsible for managing change to the underlying platform.	The provider is responsible for technical change management to the application. The consumer is responsible for changes to the user-configurable elements of the service (e.g. data types, access rights, "skinning") and associated business processes.

Problem Management	1	Problem management is a joint responsibility – problems with the underlying IaaS must be communicated and managed jointly.	Problem management is a joint responsibility – problems with the underlying PaaS must be communicated and managed jointly.	Problem management is a joint responsibility – problems with the application must be communicated and managed in a co-ordinated manner.
Vulnerability Management	1	The provider must identify and manage vulnerabilities within their IaaS. Consumers must identify and manage vulnerabilities to their hosted services (operating system and application).	The provider must identify and manage vulnerabilities within their PaaS. Consumers must identify and manage vulnerabilities to their hosted application.	The provider must identify and manage vulnerabilities within their application and supporting infrastructure.
Incident Management	1	The consumer retains primary responsibility for incident management, as the main source of incidents will usually be users, the application or underlying operating system.	Incidents may occur within the shared services or within the consumer-specific application, or some combination of the two. Consumers retain responsibility for user-initiated incidents.	The provider is responsible for managing incidents affecting their service. The consumer must still manage incidents affecting their users, data and business processes.
Respond	2			

Investigate	2			
Action	2			
Close	2			
Asset Management	1	The consumer is responsible for ensuring that they understand the assets that they have operating in the Cloud, including whether or not they hold the appropriate licenses.	The consumer is responsible for ensuring that they understand the applications that they are operating within the Cloud. The provider is responsible for ensuring that they understand their service portfolio and the underlying assets.	The provider is primarily responsible for managing the assets that provide the service.
Catalogue	2			
Configuration Management	2	The consumer has primary responsibility for configuration management of their virtual environment. The provider must provide suitable configuration management for the underlying physical hardware.	The consumer has configuration management responsibility for their deployed application. The provider has configuration management responsibility for the underlying platform and supporting physical hardware.	The provider is responsible for the configuration management of the application and supporting physical hardware. The consumer may retain responsibility for any user-configurable aspects.
License	2			

ITG RESOURCES

IT Governance Ltd. sources, creates and delivers products and services to meet the real-world, evolving IT governance needs of today's organisations, directors, managers and practitioners.

The ITG website (*www.itgovernance.co.uk*) is the international one-stop-shop for corporate and IT governance information, advice, guidance, books, tools, training and consultancy.

http://www.itgovernance.co.uk/cloud-computing.aspx is the information page on our website for our Cloud Computing resources.

Other Websites

Books and tools published by IT Governance Publishing (ITGP) are available from all business booksellers and are also immediately available from the following websites:

www.itgovernance.co.uk/catalog/355 provides information and online purchasing facilities for every currently available book published by ITGP.

http://www.itgovernance.eu is our euro-denominated website which ships from Benelux and has a growing range of books in European languages other than English.

www.itgovernanceusa.com is a US$-based website that delivers the full range of IT Governance products to North America, and ships from within the continental US.

www.itgovernanceasia.com provides a selected range of ITGP products specifically for customers in South Asia.

www.27001.com is the IT Governance Ltd. website that deals specifically with information security management, and ships from within the continental US.

Pocket Guides

For full details of the entire range of pocket guides, simply follow the links at *www.itgovernance.co.uk/publishing.aspx*.

Toolkits

ITG's unique range of toolkits includes the IT Governance Framework Toolkit, which contains all the tools and guidance that you will need in order to develop and implement an appropriate IT governance framework for your organisation. Full details can be found at *www.itgovernance.co.uk/ products/519*.

For a free paper on how to use the proprietary Calder-Moir IT Governance Framework, and for a free trial version of the toolkit, see *www.itgovernance.co.uk/calder_moir.aspx*.

There is also a wide range of toolkits to simplify implementation of management systems, such as an ISO/IEC 27001 ISMS or a BS25999 BCMS, and these can all be viewed and purchased online at: *http://www.itgovernance.co.uk/catalog/1*.

Best Practice Reports

ITG's range of Best Practice Reports is now at *www.itgovernance.co.uk/best-practice-reports.aspx*. These offer you essential, pertinent, expertly researched information on a number of key issues including Web 2.0 and Green IT.

Training Service

IT Governance offers an extensive portfolio of training courses designed to educate information security, IT governance, risk management and compliance professionals. Our classroom and online training programmes will help you develop the skills required to deliver best practice and compliance to your organisation. They will also enhance your career by providing you with industry-standard certifications and increased peer recognition. Our range of courses offers a structured learning path from foundation to advanced level in the key topics of information security, IT governance, business continuity and service management.

Full details of all IT Governance training courses can be found at *http://www.itgovernance.co.uk/training.aspx*.

Professional Services and Consultancy

IT Governance expert consultants can help you to manage the risks associated with working in the Cloud. We can analyse the gaps in your cybersecurity defences and design an appropriate set of controls that are compliant with ISO27001 best practice.

We have substantial real-world experience as a professional services company specialising in IT GRC-related management systems. Over 120 of our clients have achieved ISO27001 certification as a result of our consultancy advice and support.

Our services include delivering and mentoring a wide range of tasks, including feasibility and gap analysis, risk assessment, risk treatment plans, building and maintaining asset registers, statements of applicability, in-house training and awareness programmes, coaching and mentoring project leaders/teams, compliance audits, and recommending/applying best practice.

For more information about IT Governance Consultancy services, see: *http://www.itgovernance.co.uk/consulting.aspx*.

Newsletter

IT governance is one of the hottest topics in business today, not least because it is also the fastest moving, so what better way to keep up than by subscribing to ITG's free monthly newsletter *Sentinel*? It provides monthly updates and resources across the whole spectrum of IT governance subject matter, including risk management, information security, ITIL and IT service management, project governance, compliance and so much more. Subscribe for your free copy at: *www.itgovernance.co.uk/newsletter.aspx*.

Lightning Source UK Ltd.
Milton Keynes UK
UKOW052104240912

199558UK00005B/20/P